AF454455

מאמר הויכוח

The Kabbalist and the Philosopher

A Debate about the True Way

By

The Ramchal
Rabbi Moshe Chaim Luzzatto

Translated by
Rav Raphael Afilalo

Hazohar555@gmail.com

kabbalah5.com - zoharvideos.com – ramchal.com

YouTube: Rav Raphael Afilalo Zohar – Kabbalah

YouTube in Hebrew – רמכז הזהר

ISBN: 978-2-982217058

Publications by Rav Raphael Afilalo

English	**French**
Concepts of Kabbalah	Concepts de Kabbalah
Kabbalah Dictionary	Dictionnaire de Kabbalah
Glossary of Kabbalah	Glossaire de Kabbalah
Arizal Prince of the Kabbalists	Arizal Prince des Kabbalistes
160 Questions on the Kabbalah	160 Questions sur la Kabbalah
Kabbalah of the Arizal, according to the Ramhal	Kabbalah du Arizal, selon le Ramhal
Gates of Reincarnations	Portes des Réincarnations

Translations of books of the Ramchal

God and His Ways	Dieu et Ses Voies
The Kabbalist and the Philosopher	Le Kabbaliste et le Philosophe
The Way of the Justs	La Voie des Justes
The Wisdom of Consciousness	La Sagesse de la Conscience

בעברית

מושגי חכמת הקבלה

חשיבות לימוד הזהר

אריז״ל נשיא המקובלים

קיצור כתבי הארי

קבלה – תורה האמת

הזהר – כתבים מיסטיים של פנמיוה התורה

The life of the Ramchal

Moshe Chaim Luzzatto, known as the Ramchal, was an enigmatic figure in Jewish history, remembered as a philosopher, kabbalist, and poet whose works have had a lasting impact on Jewish thought and mysticism. Born in Padua, Italy, on April 26, 1707, into a distinguished family, Ramchal displayed prodigious intellectual capabilities from a young age.

His education was comprehensive, steeped in the dual worlds of Jewish and secular knowledge, which was a hallmark of the Italian Jewish renaissance. He was well-versed in the Torah, Talmud, and Kabbalistic literature, as well as the sciences and philosophy of his time, which informed his unique approach to Jewish theology and ethics.

The Ramchal's intellectual journey began with his study of the Talmud and other classic Jewish texts, but he was particularly drawn to the study of Kabbalah, the Jewish mystical tradition. By the age of 20, he had already begun writing his own commentaries on these subjects. His most famous work, "Mesillat Yesharim" (Path of the Just), is a systematic exploration of Jewish ethics and spiritual growth, which has become a foundational text in the Mussar movement, a Jewish ethical, educational, and cultural movement.

Despite his young age, the Ramchal's works, such as "Derech Hashem" (God and His Ways), which systematically presents the fundamentals of Jewish belief, demonstrated a mastery of Jewish law and mysticism that few could rival. He also penned "Da'at Tevunot" (The Knowing Heart), a dialogue between the intellect and the soul on the nature of God's interaction with the world, and the purpose of Creation and human existence.

However, the Ramchal's intense involvement with Kabbalah, at a time when skepticism towards mysticism was widespread following the false messianic movement of Shabbetai Zvi, aroused suspicion. His formation of a select group of disciples to study Kabbalah led to further controversy. In 1727, under communal pressure in Italy, he agreed to a ban on teaching Kabbalah and ceased writing Kabbalistic works. This period of conflict was difficult for the Ramchal, whose only desire was to elevate the spiritual state of his people.

In search of a more accommodating environment for his Kabbalistic pursuits, Ramchal left Italy in 1735, eventually settling in Amsterdam. There, he hoped to live a life of spiritual and intellectual freedom. He supported himself by working as a diamond cutter and continued to write extensively. Amsterdam's Jewish community was a center of publishing, and it was there that he printed many of his works.

The Ramchal's life in Amsterdam allowed him some respite from the controversies that had followed him in Italy, and he continued his prolific writing, including works on Hebrew grammar and logic, such as "Sefer haHigayon" (The Book of Logic), which reflected his broader academic interests.

Despite his relatively comfortable life in Amsterdam, the Ramchal's longing for the Land of Israel was intense. In 1743, he and his family made the arduous journey to the Holy Land, settling in Acre. Tragically, his time there was short-lived; he died in a plague along with his family in 1746, at the young age of 39.

The Ramchal left behind a literary legacy that spans philosophical treatises, ethical texts, kabbalistic writings, poetry, plays, and more. His works continue to be studied for their depth and insight into the human condition and the divine.

Perhaps the most enduring aspect of the Ramchal's work is his ability to synthesize the mystical and rational aspects of Judaism. He believed that an understanding of the divine structure of the universe could lead to a profound religious life rooted in ethical conduct. His works have been embraced by various streams of Jewish thought, from the rationalist to the mystic, each finding in his writings a wellspring of knowledge and inspiration.

The legacy of the Ramchal is marked by a balance between the esoteric and the practical, the heavenly and the earthly. His vision of spiritual ascent is not one of withdrawal from the world but of engagement with it, guided by divine wisdom. His life and works serve as a bridge, inviting each person to traverse the gap between the finite and infinite, between human and divine potential.

The *Maggid* of Mezritch said:
 "His generation did not merit this great man…. Many among our people, through lack of knowledge, have uttered on this saintly man calumny that was not justified."

The Gaon of Vilna declared that if Ramchal was still alive, he would have traveled to Italy on foot to learn from his wisdom.

Moshe Chaim Luzzatto's contributions to Jewish thought and his teachings are now universally recognized as treasures of Jewish literature, offering guidance to those who seek a path of righteousness, intellect, and spiritual introspection. The Ramchal remains a beacon of spiritual and moral guidance, whose influence continues to be felt centuries after his passing.

Introduction by Rav Raphael Afilalo

This book presents a fascinating dialogue between two seekers of truth and understanding of the deepest mysteries of existence - a Kabbalist, steeped in the esoteric wisdom and traditions of Jewish mysticism, and a Philosopher, representing a rational, analytical approach guided by human intellect and logic. Through their spirited exchange and debate, the profound teachings of Kabbalah are explored, questioned and ultimately validated as a true path to knowing the Divine.

The dialogue format allows the core concepts and worldview of Kabbalah to unfold in an organic way, as the Philosopher raises sincere doubts and challenges that many truth-seekers grapple with. He questions how the infinite, unchanging God can be reconciled with the Kabbalistic view of dynamic divine forces manifesting as the Sefirot. He struggles to accept the personification of these divine attributes and the elaborate mythical structure of spiritual worlds and Partsufim (configurations) that populate Kabbalistic teachings. With consummate wisdom and patience, the Kabbalist addresses each point, resolving the apparent contradictions and leading the Philosopher to a deeper understanding.

A central theme that emerges is the core purpose of creation - a divine desire to bestow ultimate goodness and fulfillment upon created beings. All the complex frameworks of spiritual forces and worlds depicted in Kabbalah are revealed as serving this singular aim. They allow for a dynamic process of human spiritual development and ultimate reward, while preserving God's absolute unity and perfection. The Kabbalist demonstrates how the entire system is founded upon deep concern for human free will and dignity.

As the dialogue progresses, it touches on many key Kabbalistic concepts: the primordial tzimtzum (contraction) of the Infinite Light to "make room" for creation; the shattering of the vessels in the "World of Points" and their reconstitution in the "World of Rectification"; the interactions of masculine and feminine divine forces; the nature of evil and its place in the divine plan; the principles of reincarnation and cosmic justice. Slowly, a majestic vision comes into focus of an awesome yet infinitely compassionate God who conceals Himself within countless veils and garments in order to guide creation in love toward its ultimate perfection.

Beyond intellectual analysis, the true study of Kabbalah is portrayed as a transformative spiritual path requiring both dedication to tradition and direct, intuitive perception of the Divine. The Kabbalist describes the meditative disciplines and practices that grant one access to ethereal realms and mystical states of consciousness. Only through such direct experience, he maintains, can one truly grasp the inner essence of the Kabbalistic teachings.

Importantly, the Kabbalist emphasizes that genuine Kabbalah is not just abstract metaphysical speculation, but a practical guide to living in alignment with divine will and attributes. It illuminates the inner meaning and spiritual power of the Mitsvot (religious deeds), imbuing physical existence with transcendent significance. A life devoted to G-d and goodness, with consciousness of the divine unity underlying all diversity, is the ultimate aim and expression of Kabbalistic wisdom.

This work, composed by the legendary mystic and thinker Rabbi Moshe Chaim Luzzatto (the Ramchal), is a rare gem of Jewish spiritual literature. It succeeds in conveying the depth, subtlety and majestic scope of Kabbalistic thought in a clear and engaging manner. The Ramchal's luminous intellect and spiritual insight shine through every page.

For anyone seeking a lucid yet profound introduction to the world of Kabbalah, there is no better entry point than The Kabbalist and the Philosopher. More than an overview of basic concepts, it captures the very spirit of the mystical quest - harmonizing mind and heart, reason and revelation, in the search for ultimate meaning. The reader is left with a sense of awe at the divine mysteries, and an unshakeable conviction in the power of Kabbalah to guide the soul's journey through an enchanted, sacred universe.

The Kabbalist and the Philosopher

Introduction by the Ramchal

The God of Israel, our Father in Heaven, who chose us to be His treasured nation, gave us this as a sign of His love, distinguishing us from all nations - the knowledge of His great Name and the secret of His wondrous deeds, which no creature can fully comprehend, except through the illumination He grants to their eyes and the effluence of His spirit upon them. As it is said: "But there is a spirit in man, and the breath of the Almighty gives them understanding" (Job 32:8), and regarding this it is stated: "He declared the power of His works to His people" (Psalms 111:6).

Since He concealed His Presence from the earth and confined it to the heavens, as the verse says: "The heavens are the heavens of the Lord" (Psalms 115:16), it follows that human beings cannot truly know or understand the workings of God, how He truthfully governs His world, but attribute everything to nature and the celestial spheres and constellations. The early heretics thought to worship the hosts of heaven in ways known to them, believing they could draw down their powers according to their manner of influence. All this stemmed from the holy Divine Presence not being revealed openly in the world, but only in a concealed manner, unlike the angels whose place is in the heavens where the Divine Presence reveals its dominion, and those standing among them know the truth hidden from the inhabitants of the earth.

However, when the Holy One, blessed be He, desired to draw near to Himself His most beloved nation, He tore open the heavens and revealed to them His mysteries, until they all knew with certainty that all governance of the lower realms, in every detail imaginable, is solely in the hands of the Divine Presence. There is no small matter in the world that is not dependent on lofty and exalted matters. They then knew and understood the entire secret of creation: for what purpose the world was created, on what it stands, in what manner it is conducted, and the ultimate end of all these things.

They perceived the profound simplicity of the blessed One, and the great creations He made for His own honor. They also saw how the people of this world walk in darkness, with the truth concealed from their eyes, and how in this world, the Holy One, blessed be He, left stumbling blocks for the wicked. For since He is hidden from the people of this world, He gave the Satan permission to roam the earth and traverse it, to act and entice the hearts of men with various kinds of deceit and falsehood, so that the human heart is lured after them and errs in many fallacies, thinking the world operates solely according to the visible laws of nature.

The Holy One, blessed be He, revealed all these matters before their eyes. They saw and grasped them in truth, along with the reason for it all - the profound supernal counsel wisely orchestrating everything to its ultimate purpose. Here they beheld the greatness of the Torah and Mitsvot, their significance, and how they bring about great effects throughout all of creation. They saw on what all the details of the Mitsvot depend, how absolutely necessary they are, as our Sages said: "Between each utterance - the details and specificities of the Torah" (Shir HaShirim Rabbah 5, Jerusalem Talmud Shekalim 6:1). Regarding all this, Moses declared to them: "To you it was shown, that you might know that the Lord, He is God; there is none else beside Him" (Deuteronomy 4:35).

For the Holy One, blessed be He, showed them all of existence, what it stands upon, and they knew with certainty that He alone governs, with no other power - not natural, not random, nor in any other way - only the governance that He, may He be blessed, conducts with the profound counsel He revealed to them. He commanded them, as it is written, to set this truth in their hearts, that it should be settled within them without any doubt, just as they saw it with utter clarity.

This is what He said to them: "Know this day, and lay it to your heart..." (ibid. 4:39). All these things they saw at the time of the giving of the Torah, as it is written: "Behold, the Lord our God has shown us His glory..." (ibid. 5:21). Therefore, He commanded them that just as they saw with their own eyes, so should they transmit it to their children and grandchildren for generations. This is what He said to them: "Only take heed to yourself, and keep your soul diligently, lest you forget the things which your eyes have seen, and lest they depart from your heart all the days of your life; but make them known to your children and your children's children" (ibid. 4:9). He does not say "which you heard" but rather "which your eyes have seen," indicating that He speaks of what they saw with their own eyes. He later explains: "The day that you stood before the Lord your God in Horeb..." and do not think that regarding "You saw no manner of form" He is only negating their seeing an image, for then He would have said "the thing which your eyes saw." Rather, the truth is that they saw something of the supernal glory, as He says later: "Behold, the Lord our God has shown us His glory and His greatness..." (ibid. 5:21). It is to this that Moses himself attests, as it is written: "To you it was shown..." (ibid. 4:35), "Know this day, and lay it to your heart..." (ibid. 4:39), and it is regarding this that He warns and commands them: "Lest you forget... but make them known to your children and your children's children" (ibid. 4:9).

For this is what Israel knows, which the other nations do not know at all, because Israel merited to see all this at Mount Sinai, which the nations of the world did not see. The nations of the world can only engage in what human intellect allows. As I wrote above, the Holy One, blessed be He, wanted to hide His Presence from the lower realms and He erected a separating screen before them, so they could not see the truth and where the matters of this world are rooted and suspended. However, one time the Holy One, blessed be He, desired and tore this screen before all Israel, until He established them upon His truth. From then on, these matters remained sealed in their hearts, and they have the commandment to teach them, each man to his son.

Furthermore, from there they merited to establish prophets who would continually renew this knowledge within them. Throughout the era of the prophets, this knowledge was widespread in Israel, in everyone's mouths, as is stated in the Zohar, Leviticus: "What a difference between the earlier generations and the later generations" (beginning of Vayikra), see there. For this is Israel's portion from God, "This is the heritage of the servants of the Lord, and their righteousness is of Me" (Isaiah 54:17) - to fathom His counsel and know His great deeds performed according to His wondrous wisdom, as the verse states: "How great are Your works, O Lord! You have made them all with wisdom; the earth is full of Your creations" (Psalms 104:24). The entire secret is encapsulated in these words: "The earth is full of Your creations," as I will further explain ahead in the essay.

When our iniquities caused the Holy One, blessed be He, to drive us away from His glorious and splendid House, "woe" became solely an expression of anguish (Megillah 10b), for "He has crushed me in a place of jackals, and covered me with deep darkness" (Psalms 44:20), "He has made me dwell in dark places, as those that have been long dead" (Lamentations 3:6). Then wisdom began to depart from Israel, as the darkness grew progressively thicker due to the intensifying evil day by day. Israel sank deeper and deeper into this great darkness throughout the generations. They found themselves distant from the holy Divine Presence - not distant in essence, for Israel's sanctity never changes for all eternity, as it is said of them: "The children of Israel, a people near unto Him" (Psalms

148:14); rather, the darkness obscured them, making it impossible for them to gaze at the light, even though it is close to them, and therefore they are called distant from it.

However, God in His mercy left us a remnant, which is the simple meaning of the Torah, given to us as an eternal heritage that will never depart from our mouths. By virtue of this, we remain constantly close to Him, if not overtly, then at least in a concealed manner. Regarding this it is said: "And He said: 'I will hide My face from them, I will see what their end shall be'" (Deuteronomy 32:20) - although He hides, He still sees. But it is a great hardship for the souls, which yearn to bask in the light of life in His nearness and to fathom His counsel, for they were created to be lacking this light. As is stated in Ra'aya Meheimna, Parshat Pinchas (249a): Rabbi Shimon said: "Woe to those who eat the straw of the Torah and do not know the secrets of the Torah, but only the light matters and the simple meanings of the Torah." See there, for this matter requires extensive explanation, and here is not the place. However, as the exile lengthened, this knowledge diminished greatly. In these final generations, only a minute amount remains of it. In the early generations, this wisdom was exceedingly great, as you can see in the words of the holy Zohar - how they stand at the pinnacle of the world and expound upon the mysteries of the King Himself, interpreting upon each letter many profound secrets that impart great wisdom into the counsel of the blessed One. But in our generations, all that remains is but a memory of the wisdom that existed in previous generations. Were it not for the holy Rabbi Isaac Luria (the Arizal), of blessed memory, who opened gates of light for us with his holy spirit, the wisdom would have been completely forgotten by us.

Even now, after that righteous, eternal foundation (the Arizal) ascended to his rest, the wisdom became increasingly concealed, generation after generation, until his words and matters remained like the words of a sealed book, with many difficulties and contradictions found in the teachings of Rabbi Chaim Vital, of blessed memory.

What is even more difficult is that the overall understanding of the matters is very cryptic and sealed, for the Arizal, of blessed memory, intentionally obscured his words extensively and did not want to explain in writing. This caused the readers of his words to take them at face value and superficially, which is not real understanding at all. We are left with mere names of concepts that need to be memorized like a table of contents, knowing that there are so many sefirot, so many Partsufim, so many worlds, that they are garbed within each other, that there are so many ascents and descents - but we do not know the meaning behind all these things and what they signify. It turns out that this is not knowledge at all, but just memorization of terminology without any real comprehension. The Arizal himself warned about this in his explanation of the Discourse on the Paces, stating: "However, the reader should not think that with this explanation, he can understand even the touch of an ear of grain of this entire teaching, for even if he would live a thousand years, he would not even begin one introduction."

End quote. (Shaar Maamarei Razal, Midrash Rabbah, Parsha 43).

Now, with the wisdom remaining so bare - obscure matters without understanding - another problem arose. Great sages pushed it into a corner, for it is the nature of sages to seek well-grounded comprehension, to know matters in depth and not be satisfied with empty words. Seeing that these matters did not fulfill them, they said, why should we waste our time on what we cannot grasp. Others did worse, not only despising it but even slandering it, considering it foolishness that people accepted upon themselves to be enslaved by coarse and unacceptable things. They went so far as to deny its fundamentals and negate the holy Zohar being composed by Rabbi Shimon bar Yochai, of blessed memory, and his colleagues. All this because the words of the wisdom seemed strange in their eyes, to the point that they deemed them unworthy of being attributed to the mighty founding pillars, the Tannaim, of blessed memory. But the truth is that the wisdom is very concealed, and regarding this it is said: From the mouths of scribes and not from books (Gittin 60b), for the Arizal, of blessed memory, intended to hide his words in a book and left the secret sealed in his treasuries, to reveal to whomever he deemed fit. With the students understanding only from the book, the "scribes" (sages) have ceased from the world, until today the wisdom is confused in the hands of its learners, and few are those who plumb the depths of the matters and see the beauty of the wisdom not at all.

Therefore, I said to my heart: "It is time to act for the Lord" (Psalms 119:126), and this matter does not require embarrassment or shame to say: Who am I to come this far, to speak before those greater and better than I... for there is a time and season for every purpose, and the verse states: "I will speak of Your testimonies before kings and will not be ashamed" (Psalms 119:46), for it is Torah, and we need to learn to bring gratification to our Maker. The crown of Torah is accessible; whoever wishes to merit it can come and merit it. It is no small thing to me - to bask in the light of life, in the secrets of the Torah which are the radiant garments of the Divine Presence, and in His sanctuary which is entirely proclaiming His glory. Moreover, all the details and intricacies of the Torah depend on it, and those things that seem trivial to the eyes, which do not shine with this great light - all the protective measures instituted by the Sages, their decrees and stringencies that people trample with their heels - it is specifically through this wisdom that we know and see how far-reaching these matters are and how they all stand at the summit of the world.

Therefore, I chose to arrange this essay in an orderly and pleasing structure to reveal the beauty of this great wisdom to the eyes of the children of Israel. Since philosophy and rationalism have always been a constant adversary to this great wisdom, like a brazen maidservant seeking to supplant her mistress - it is the leprosy that has truly spread, due to our many sins, among Israel, becoming a stumbling block of iniquity for them, ensnaring people who consider themselves wise and lovers of knowledge.

For when they delight in its facade, as it masquerades in garments attractive to the eye, and how appealing they are to the eyes - all seemingly well-grounded ideas, acceptable to the intellect with decisive proofs and choice reasons, with charm that is deceptive and beauty that is vain - it shows them that the true wisdom is nothing at all. For it guards its forehead (identity) only for its masters, black on the outside and comely on the inside, fulfilling the verse "Do not look upon me, that I am swarthy" (Song of Songs 1:6). Therefore, I arranged this essay in the form of a debate between a rationalist and a kabbalist, in which all the claims made by these rationalists against this holy wisdom will be presented, along with their refutations in the words of the kabbalist responding to the rationalist's arguments.

I proceeded in the order of the debate from the premise to its implication, as is fitting for an intellect that settles upon matters in order, and I divided it into eight debates:

In the first will come all the major difficulties that ostensibly fall upon the entirety of the wisdom according to the words of the kabbalists, of blessed memory, and their resolutions, all explained well.

The second will clarify the entire "tree" of the sefirot, Partsufim, and worlds, from the first to the last level, meaning from the beginning of Adam Kadmon until the end of all the worlds, as transmitted to us from the Arizal, of blessed memory.

The third will explain the overall purpose of this entire "tree" with all its branches in a concise manner, covering the essential aim of the wisdom in all its investigations.

The fourth will elaborate on all the details of the "tree" at length, examining each concept with all the necessary distinctions.

The fifth is the order for teaching beginners in this wisdom. Whoever wishes to study in the proper order should start with this last debate, then proceed to the second debate, then the third, and then the fourth. For I followed the order of the debate to align with the path of the essay that I chose. Know, pleasant reader, that the words of the wisdom of truth are either understood with the utmost clarity, appearing as clear as the sun itself, or they are not understood at all and are utterly foreign. For one who follows them in the straight path will find them as clear as a word can be, all being necessary matters, each word upon its wheels, without any doubt whatsoever. But for one who errs and mistakes the true path, they will appear as lofty mountains that cannot be ascended at all. As they said in the Zohar, Parshat Pinchas (253b): "The Faithful Shepherd said: These words, how sealed they are to one who does not know them, yet revealed to one who knows them."

Just as one who studies them without proper understanding finds them like unseasoned bread, one who studies them with understanding will find in them profound wisdom, before which all other wisdoms will be considered as naught and void. His heart will be ignited with love for the holy Divine Presence, to desire His ways, to live only to find favor in His eyes, and to bring satisfaction to his Maker. "Happy is the people who have it so; happy is the people whose God is the Lord" (Psalms 144:15). However, be in awe, trembling, and shaking, and let them not depart from you. With a clear mind, set the matters aright in your heart, "that you may give wisdom from your mouth, knowledge and understanding" (Proverbs 2:6). "But it is a spirit in man, and the breath of the Almighty gives them understanding" (Job 32:8).

Part One - The Need for the Wisdom of Kabbalah

Philosopher: Peace be upon you, my brother! How good is your coming at this time, for I am in great need of you.

Kabbalist: How can a philosopher need a kabbalist? You have already let your thoughts roam all corners of creation and subjugated it under you with your decisive proofs. How can I be of use to you?

Philosopher: Excessive praise is nothing but mockery. Let us come to the matter at hand. I will speak to you with the integrity of my heart, as is the way of our friendship. I have read and heard some matters from your Kabbalah, and they seem quite strange to me, for they contradict my investigations entirely. However, since I saw many pious individuals who followed its ways, I said to myself that I would see what you have to say. Perhaps I will hear from you something that, if not compelling, will at least not be contradictory and foolish according to sound reason, as it currently appears to me, leaving me no choice but to reject it.

Kabbalist: I will do as you say and inform you of the truth as it was transmitted to us by those who know the truth. The entire benefit of this knowledge will be that you receive from me another piece of knowledge: that you know that all a person can grasp through his philosophical inquiry is considered as nothing compared to what he can grasp through the true Kabbalah. Regarding this, the wise one said: "For the Lord gives wisdom, from His mouth come knowledge and understanding" (Proverbs 2:6). Now open your mouth wide, and I will fill it.

Philosopher: First, I wish to know from you about the sefirot that you mention - what are they? I would like to know this clearly, for I have heard such strange things about them that I had to restrain myself out of respect from crying out in the streets how astonished I was by them. I was nearly forced to say that they are nonsensical matters.

Kabbalist: Tell me what you heard about this.

Philosopher: I heard it said that they are one light that the Emanator, blessed be He, emanated from His primordial light, and that He, blessed be He, garbs Himself within them like a soul within a body.

Kabbalist: What else did you hear about this?

Philosopher: I heard that there is Atzilut, and there is Beriah, Yetzirah, and Asiyah. The difference between them is that Beriah, Yetzirah, and Asiyah are nothing but an illumination from this emanated light that we mentioned, and that it is divided into two parts. The inner part of it, meaning the soul, is called Divinity, while from the soul and below it is no longer called Divinity, but rather the "World of Separation." This applies to all three worlds.

Kabbalist: What do you say about this?

Philosopher: By the life of my soul, I do not even know how to arrange my difficulties due to their great quantity and quality, for this contradicts all reason and the truth of our faith.

Kabbalist: How so?

Four Difficulties Regarding the Sefirot of Atzilut

Philosopher: From now on, you will not escape one of these two options: Either you will say that they are Divinity, or not.

Kabbalist: But you already heard about this, that Atzilut is Divinity.

Philosopher: If it is Divinity, how can you conceive in your mind that Divinity can be derived from Divinity?

You said two things - that this contradicts all reason and our faith.

Philosopher: Indeed, regarding reason, it is as I said. For how can it be conceived that Divinity derives from Divinity? For God, meaning that Unique One who must exist to be the head of all creatures - since they are many, it is impossible for them to be conducted in an equal and fixed order except by a single head over them all. Therefore, we must understand that Unique One as the ultimate unity. How can we conceive of plurality, birth, and derivation of light within Him?

As for faith, tell me now, is this notion so far, God forbid, from the belief of the Christians, who posited the Trinity, saying that He is three and He is one? For the One actually derives progeny from Himself, and yet it is all one. Furthermore, that which is renewed must not have existed prior to its renewal. If you say that the sefirot are new divinity, while the Infinite is ancient divinity, is this not exactly what is said about such things: "They chose new gods" (Judges 5:8)?

Additionally, how greatly do you stumble in faith, for we know that the Holy One, blessed be He, is absolutely simple, unaffected by any bodily contingencies. According to your words, there is no greater contingency than this - that His essence, blessed be He, should transform from non-existence to existence.

Kabbalist: You have already shaken the entire world with your words. Do you have any more such difficulties?

Philosopher: Indeed, I do. For now I spoke in general only about the matter of Atzilut. When we come to Beriah, Yetzirah, and Asiyah - they are exceedingly numerous. In truth, I have such strong questions and difficulties there that no mind of a wise and understanding person can bear them.

Kabbalist: Please state your words, and let me know what you have to say about this.

Difficulties Regarding the Sefirot of Beriah, Yetzirah, Asiyah

Philosopher: When you come to Beriah, Yetzirah, Asiyah, you make a continuum, and still call it Divinity. Afterward, you say that part of it is called Divinity, while part of it is not called by this name. Tell me, by your life, have you ever heard that Divinity could be divided to such an extent that half of it remains Divinity while half of it does not, but rather becomes a subservient slave to the first half? Believe me, faithful friend, these are not words of wisdom. It is impossible to bring such matters to the ears of an intelligent person, only to the simple-minded who believe everything.

However, there are two things I would like to know in any case: First, who involved us in this conflict? Second, what benefit emerges from this knowledge? Is the faith that the entire congregation of Israel believes - that the Creator is One, that He governs His world, that He gave His Torah to us, and that our Messiah will come - not good? What need do we have for all these matters of sefirot and worlds that breed nothing but confusion?

Kabbalist: Please complete your words.

Philosopher: I have one difficulty that encompasses all difficulties - that everything I have read or heard is astonishing from beginning to end. However, I think that if I would find at least one solid foundation upon which all these structures could be built, then perhaps the details would be comprehensible. But without that, why should I toil over the details when the entirety is difficult?

Can a Body Develop from Divinity?

However, I will not refrain from mentioning one strong difficulty I have with their words, which branches into two, but has one root:

I heard that you say that the sefirot developed level by level until this physical world came into being. This is an extremely difficult matter. What sense can there be to these words? How can that which is Divinity develop to the point of becoming one opaque body?

How Can We Understand the Emergence of the Other Side from Holiness?

The second, an even greater and more astounding difficulty, is what they say - that the Other Side emerged from the end of din (justice). Even more astonishing, they say that initially, good and evil were mixed together, and that is why the first worlds were destroyed, until the good was clarified by itself, which are the sefirot of holiness, and the evil by itself, which are the sefirot of the Other Side. To me, this matter seems almost like heresy, God forbid - to say that the Other Side was initially mixed into the sefirot, whether overtly or covertly. Say what you will, but they were one entity. How can one thing be clarified from it, with one part becoming the sefirot, which is Divinity, and the other part becoming the Other Side? I have no heart to accept these matters, and certainly not to utter them, for it seems to me that this leads to the heresy of two authorities, God forbid.

If the Sefirot are Divinity, How Can They Emanate from Divinity?

If you answer that the sefirot are light emanated from the Blessed Infinite One, and that is why such things are possible for them, this was already the first difficulty - how can one say that Divinity emanates from Divinity? If they are emanated from Him, they are outside of Him. Even if you say a hundred times that they are like a flame connected to a coal (Sefer Yetzirah 1:7), these are things said by mouth but are not accepted by the heart. For to say that something that is not essentially divine could still be divine is one of the impossibilities.

How Can We Understand Service Via the Sefirot?
Furthermore, according to your approach, all service is via the sefirot, and I see no permissibility for this. For we cannot escape the following: If they are not Divinity itself, then they must be able to be separate from Him and exist as vessels without light, like a body without a soul. Yet they are still described with the very attributes of Divinity - this is improper. For "the God of gods is the Lord" (Psalms 50:1), meaning the Holy One, blessed be He. According to your ways, it would mean Chesed, Gevurah, Tiferet. According to our faith, it is impossible to use these names for anyone other than the Emanator, blessed be He. Rather, "You shall have no other gods before Me" (Exodus 20:3). If you answer that Divinity cleaves to them to such an extent that they are called by His name - such a thing should never be uttered, for you would be giving an opening to heretics, God forbid, and even worse.

In summary, these matters are very perplexing. Now, if you have the means to resolve them, if not entirely, then at least some of them, I would rejoice greatly.

Kabbalist: Until now, you have made yourself the witness, the judge, and the litigant. I, too, like you, will place you between Him and me as the adjudicator. Your reason will be the one I anticipate, as will you. But incline your ear and set aside your desire for just a moment, until you receive the true knowledge with a clear mind. Indeed, it requires resolution and conciliation.

Philosopher: Speak, and I shall listen.

Kabbalist: You are mistaken in every respect.

Philosopher: But I have heard many of your Kabbalists speak the very things I said.

Kabbalist: Their words need to be properly understood, not taken superficially.

Philosopher: Now let me hear a clear explanation from you.

This Wisdom Teaches the Unity of God and the Integrity of His Governance with Great Wisdom

Kabbalist: The foundation of this entire wisdom is the unity of the Emanator, blessed be He, that He is one in every way, without any change, plurality, or bodily contingency whatsoever.

Philosopher: The foundation is very good, if it can bear its structure.

Kabbalist: The entire matter of the wisdom of Kabbalah is nothing but an explanation of the attribute of His justice, blessed be He, the order of the laws of governance - how the Holy One, blessed be He, causes and governs all affairs of His world with great wisdom.

Philosopher: If this is what we would find in this wisdom, we would find something great. However, I do not see this wisdom proceeding along this path.

How Can We Understand Development in the Sefirot?

Kabbalist: Did I not tell you that you are mistaken in every respect?

Philosopher: I am stating what I gathered from the matters I read in your texts. I saw that you want to explain the chain of development - how the created being emerges from the Creator, as if the Creator, blessed be He, is the primary substance of the creations, developing from Him Himself. This primary substance gradually develops until it reaches the creations themselves. These are the sefirot and all that you expound upon regarding them. For you say that the Creator, blessed be He, placed His very name and was affected in one way until His own light was found to be affected and progressively developing until the lowest level was found. Now, if this matter could truly be stated, it would be very nice. For this development would certainly be the cause of all existences, and their variations would cause the variations in the world's affairs. Therefore, it would be good to know it, especially since the matter lends itself to attributing to it all the Mitsvot and service, for it needs to be ordered according to its good nature. However, as I prefaced, if it could be said - for how can it be said that the light of the Creator, blessed be He, is affected or develops? You yourself have already admitted that contingencies do not apply to the Emanator, blessed be He.

Kabbalist: I acknowledge all this, and on the contrary, this is the foundation of my entire structure - that the Emanator, blessed be He, is not subject to any bodily contingency. But I said that you are mistaken in every respect, and I repeat it. It is impossible to say in any way that His light, blessed be He, is itself affected and develops to the extent that the Creator becomes a creation. Have you never heard that creation is something from nothing? If so, how can development and affectedness be spoken of?

Philosopher: Yes, your words have added water, now see to it that you add flour.

Understanding This Wisdom is Knowing His Governance, Blessed Be He

Kabbalist: But you will see that it is impossible for great sages to err in this, such as those from whom the Kabbalah flows to us. However, I will demonstrate to you that you did not understand anything of what you read. Do you know how to explain these levels mentioned in the sefirot, and all their variations mentioned at all times, what their benefit is in creation? How action and deed will result from them below? But inform me of the details, not generalities. If you know this, you can say that you understood what you read. If not, you will certainly say that you read what you did not understand.

Philosopher: Yes, in general I tell you that they are all matters needed to bring about the development of the world, and that through their differences in their states, they differentiate the affairs of the world. But in particular, I do not know what they are - not the qav (line) or the reshimu (impression), not Adam Kadmon, nor his worlds, the tikunim (rectifications) of the Partsufim (configurations) and their garments and intervals - all these are numerous. These are things I have read but do not know their nature. I only see great difficulties in them.

Kabbalist: If so, you do not know. I will start you on one path so you may see what you had not considered in these matters.

Philosopher: Speak.

Infinite and Sefirot - What He Can Will and What He Willed

Kabbalist: The Emanator, blessed be He, is certainly the Master of will, according to what He willed and wills. Now we can speak of Him in two aspects: in terms of His essence and in terms of His will. Do you admit this or not?

Philosopher: Certainly, we can speak about any subject in terms of each aspect of it independently. For example, when speaking about a person's affairs, the person is called the subject of the discussions, meaning the qualities being discussed about him are called the aspect or aspects of him. We can discuss an aspect of the person - that he is learned, charitable, or wise. Each of these is an independent aspect that we can discuss regarding each subject on its own.

Kabbalist: Regarding the essence of the Emanator, blessed be He, we are forbidden to speak of it, and we do not even need to delve into it at all. For it suffices us to know of His existence. When we know that He is the ultimate perfection, that He is omnipotent - we know what we need to know in this matter. Beyond this, we are already forbidden to even speak. Therefore, we will no longer speak of His essence, only of His will, for this is closer to us and is permissible, as we are not touching upon His essence at all.

Philosopher: It is good to speak of His will. But what can you say? His will has no end, His thought has no limit. What can you investigate regarding that which has no bounds or finitude?

Kabbalist: This is precisely what I wanted to elicit from you, that you admit that there is no end to His will and thought. From now on, you will not be able to flee from me concerning what I wish to impart to you. Please tell me, you certainly believe in reward and punishment, for it is one of the fundamentals of faith. But tell me: There are deeds in the world for which the Holy One, blessed be He, desires to benefit their doers, and there are those for which He desires to punish. There is a time when He elevates and a time when He lowers; a time when He impoverishes and a time when He enriches. If so, in His will there is certainly a will of beneficence, a will of harm, a will of lowering, and a will of elevating. All this is certainly in order, for there is an order to the governance. If so, we can certainly discuss all of this, as we are not touching upon His essence, blessed be He, at all. In summary, these are the attributes of His will that we can certainly investigate and know.

Philosopher: Yes, regarding all these we can contemplate. Of them it is said: "These are but the fringes of His ways" (Job 26:14).

Kabbalist: You have spoken well. Now, tell me, could He have created the world only in the manner in which He created it? You cannot say this, for He could have created it with one utterance (Avot 5:1), yet He created it with ten utterances. Or will you say that He could only create as many creatures as He did create and no more, or in the form that He created them and no more? You cannot say any of this, for you also admit that He is omnipotent. If so, when we come to contemplate this will of His, blessed be He, we find that He is omnipotent without any bounds or limits. Yet, we find that He now acts with finitude and performs a limited action according to the service of man, for the generality subsists through the particulars. The creation of the world, too, was only in the boundary He desired, not according to His omnipotence and infinity. For if He would create according to His omnipotence and infinity, the creations would also be without end. If so, we certainly say that there are two things we must understand regarding this will of His - what He can will and what He willed. What He can will is without measure or end, while what He willed is in the measure and boundary He desired. Do you agree with all this?

Philosopher: True, certainly. This is a reality that cannot be denied.

5Kabbalist: Now we must assign names to these levels, so that we can discuss them. For without names, it is impossible to discuss the subjects, to properly distinguish them from each other. The names the Kabbalists assigned to these two aspects are: Infinite and Sefirot.

The Infinite, blessed be He, is the will according to what He was able to will, which has no end, measure or limit; the sefirot are what He willed in a finite way, included in specific attributes that He desired. For example, let us say: compassion, anger and the like; kindness, judgment and mercy in all their specific conditions. These are what we call sefirot, meaning the attributes of will - not those that are His in essence, for He is omnipotent, but rather those that He willed to create His world with and through, and to guide them in order and limit. We do not speak at all of His omnipotence, for we have no engagement with or knowledge of it, and we are forbidden to engage with it, as it is said: "Do not inquire into that which is too wondrous for you" (Chagigah 13a, based on Ben Sira), for the intellect can only investigate what it can grasp. The limited intellect cannot grasp the unlimited, so it should desist. But the specific and limited attributes that the will itself desired - those are what we seek and understand, for we understand the matter of these attributes, how this creation emerges through them, how it is conducted by them, what their purpose is, and how the Mitsvot reach and align with them. In summary, the entire matter of governance, wherever it may be, depends entirely upon them.

Philosopher: Your words are good, and I am settled with this matter. Moreover, these premises are certainly necessary and cannot be denied. However, I still do not believe that you can complete the wisdom with this, for I do not yet see an opening to introduce the difficult and strange matters I found. Furthermore, your words trouble me, for you say that the sefirot are lights, but what you are saying does not mean lights.

Infinite and Sefirot are Called Lights

Kabbalist: Will in general is called illumination. The Infinite, blessed be He, is called simple light, so in this sense, the powers of will and its attributes are called lights.

Philosopher: This is called speaking metaphorically, which means that these things have no actual existence, only conceptual.

Kabbalist: Now you are mistaken even in your own philosophical inquiry. I will tell you this as a general introduction to all matters of wisdom: One who wishes to understand the matters of the sefirot must envision the human soul and its aspects. The soul is not merely a conceptual matter, but an actual power. True, it is subtle and does not fall under the senses, but it is still a power, and all the faculties and attributes it comprises are actual things within it, not metaphorical, and they are real matters that exist in its law.

Now understand this above: The existence of the Emanator, blessed be He, is undoubtedly certain. His will certainly has existence, and it is His illumination, for illumination is what the luminous essence radiates and sends forth from itself. So too, illumination refers to what the Unique Master wills, but this is said to be simple illumination, meaning not like this lowly light which is physical, while He, blessed be He, is beyond all physicality. Rather, simple light means light in the sense that it is similar to the concept of light, but as it is - simple, distinct from the essence of our light, and the powers of this will are all lights, and they are actual matters, just as they are in the soul itself. They are the powers of the will that bring about effects in the world.

Philosopher: The matter is good. In summary: The sefirot are the powers of the supreme, limited will - those that He willed, according to which all actions occur. Complete your words on the matter of Beriah, Yetzirah, and Asiyah.

Sefirot of Atzilut - Powers of Will Alone; Sefirot of Beriah, Yetzirah, Asiyah - Powers of Will with Angels

Kabbalist: The supreme will, blessed be He, desired to perform His deeds through His emissaries, meaning the angels. His illumination stands over His emissaries so they may perform their tasks. We must now speak of two things: His will, blessed be He, and its powers according to the order of His governance; and how He stands over His emissaries and in what manner He stands over them as they carry out the actions of His decrees. This is Atzilut and Beriah, Yetzirah, Asiyah.

Atzilut is the totality of all the limited powers of His will that we mentioned, meaning the sefirot in all the details of their arrangements, and they are nothing but powers of His will. Therefore, Atzilut is said to be Divinity in all its parts. Meaning, for all the categories of matters we discuss, one world is called, and it turns out that Atzilut is the world of Divinity alone, which are the powers of governance, nothing more.

Beriah, Yetzirah, Asiyah are other categories, meaning other worlds, in the sense we mentioned, which are the matter of standing of the Creator, blessed be He, over His created emissaries, to do what needs to be done. Just as Atzilut is a category of the powers of will alone, so Beriah, Yetzirah, Asiyah are the powers of will with those receiving from them. Thus,

Beriah, Yetzirah, Asiyah are worlds built of two things: the illumination overseeing its emissaries and standing over them, and the emissaries acting according to its command. This category is found to be built of these two things together, and is not complete with one of them alone.

When we then go on to evaluate the types of this category in relation to each other, we will call the entire illumination of the Divinity, blessed be He, the soul of that world. To all the divisions of the servants, we will call spirit and soul in relation to the illumination over them. These divisions are according to the arrangements that order all matters of governance in the secret of soul, spirit, soul. This is not the place to explain this, for it depends on knowing the specific orders of governance. Even the illumination of Divinity itself which we call soul, when we come to discern the details of itself alone, we will also divide into soul, spirit, soul. But when dividing the types under the category, one need not be concerned with the details of the type, only the types themselves are evaluated in relation to each other. In this way, we say that Divinity is the soul in Beriah, Yetzirah, Asiyah, while spirit and soul are the separated beings - not that it is all one essence, with the soul in it remaining Divinity while the spirit and soul become separate, but rather they are two essences. One is called soul and the other is called spirit and soul in relation to it, like the soul to the body, which are two essences, with the body being a separate matter from the soul.

Philosopher: Good and fine. We now have two subjects to discuss: the governance of the supreme thought and its arrangements, and the standing of Divinity, blessed be He, over His emissaries to bring about His actions. This is Atzilut and this is Beriah, Yetzirah, Asiyah. But please tell me: Why do you say that the sefirot of Beriah, Yetzirah, Asiyah are lesser than those of Atzilut, and likewise those of Yetzirah are lesser than Beriah, and those of Asiyah lesser than Yetzirah?

The Gradation of Revelations in the Worlds of Beriah, Yetzirah, Asiyah

Kabbalist: It is simple - the Divine Presence rests upon an angel only according to its power, and as the levels of the angels vary, so this indwelling varies from great power to small power. Therefore, all of Beriah, Yetzirah, Asiyah are found to be lesser than Atzilut, for it is the power alone, while Beriah, Yetzirah, Asiyah are the emissaries, and the supernal powers are not revealed upon the angels in their great power, only according to what the angels can receive. Beriah, Yetzirah, Asiyah are lesser, each lower one than its higher, for the revelation of the indwelling above is greater than below. When we evaluate this revelation of the indwelling, we find three revelations, each lesser than the other, meaning that of Yetzirah is lesser than Beriah, and Asiyah lesser than Yetzirah. Each revelation is comprised of ten levels, which are the ten sefirot of Beriah, Yetzirah, Asiyah.

The Sefirot - The Powers that are the Roots of the Created Beings

I will further tell you a great principle: The Emanator, blessed be He, in His infinite essence, has no comparison at all with the creatures He created, and in His omnipotence He could have created them all in other ways that contain many opposites. However, it was a decree before Him to equate His action with what is acted upon by it, in the manner that people use great power for a difficult thing and small power for an easy thing. So too, the supreme will, as it were, desired to act with great power in big, important matters, and with small power in small matters, even though He does not need this. Regarding this they said: "But He could have created it with one utterance! Rather, in order to exact payment from the wicked who destroy the world that was created with ten utterances, and to give ample reward to the righteous who sustain the world that was created with ten utterances" (Avot 5:1). For we see with our own eyes that He wanted each type of creature to have its own utterance, and with one utterance He did not create two things. This was to align and equate the action with what was acted upon.

Here the entirety of this wisdom of truth is rooted: to distinguish the powers with which the Holy One, blessed be He, created His world - what their powers are, their measures, the relation between one power and another, and between one created being and another. For since the powers were limited to will only these and no others - we certainly know them. This is because the Holy One, blessed be He, certainly created His world according to one intention, and according to this intention, He limited and arranged the types of powers He wants to invest in this matter, and decreed the order between them, the relations and the laws. This is something a person can understand when it happens to him, since it is not something unlimited that goes beyond the law of human intellect. The entirety of this entire order is this wisdom. That is why we evaluate in it, in stages, the measures of these powers, and understand how things depend on each other, and how the created beings are bound together. The main point is to understand that for each created thing, there is a root of its own in the powers, all in gradation and order, so that they are all interconnected and aligned toward a single intention alone.

Philosopher: These matters are certainly good and necessary, for we have seen this - the matter of the ten utterances that are distinct from each other. Each utterance was made a beginning for the creature decreed by that utterance. When the utterances are discerned, there is a beginning for all the types of creatures. From this we learn that there is a specific beginning for each matter on its own. Since the matters are in their essence bound and united according to the ultimate intention, the beginning of them proceeds first in this gradation and order, followed by the creatures emerging from it. We now have the distinction of all the lights mentioned in the wisdom.

I have one more thing to ask of you, if you have a tradition about it: Why did the supreme will need or want to make a distinct beginning for the creatures, and what is the benefit in this?

Each Creature Has Its Own Root

Kabbalist: These words you spoke have no explanation. Do you think the world and its creatures were made without an ultimate intention? You must perforce admit that there is one intention for all that was created. I suppose you will not ask now why there are so many creatures, no less and no more, for this is what is needed to arrive at this intention - all these things with all their conditions. Is it not necessary now that there be a distinct beginning for each creature in the supreme thought, in the supreme light, which are all one? Each creature exists because its fellow is not sufficient without it to do what is needed according to the ultimate intention. If so, each matter certainly has its own beginning.

And you will further understand this matter: Here the service of man is understood, along with reward and punishment. For since there is a beginning for each created matter on its own, the supreme will desired and made the sustenance of that thing, the action of that beginning, dependent on man's choice for good through the act of one Mitsvah. One who fulfills one Mitsvah is found to cause that specific beginning upon which the Mitsvah depends to perform its action well. The Creator, blessed be He, who created it, knows to divide the types of these beginnings into the distinctions He desired, and to give Mitsvot that depend on these types for them to fulfill for good. He told and passed these acts to Israel whom He chose for His service.

The reason for all the Mitsvot and all their conditions is according to the beginning they depend on. The supreme thought aligned and coordinated all that is necessary according to choice, for the sake of reward and punishment, for the sake of the world's sustenance at all times, and for all cycles of things, until all of created existence will be perfected in its entirety. He decreed powers for all this, and from these powers, existences came into being. These are the lights, which are lights because they are powers of the supreme will, which is light. However, it is called simple light, meaning unrevealed and utterly unseen. The sefirot are lights whose matter He wanted to reveal more, and also to reveal their light to the created beings, or to the angels, or to the souls, in the sense of what they said: "And they delight in the radiance of the Divine Presence."

Philosopher: It is the way of the wise to admit the truth. I, in my days, never thought of the Kabbalists as anything but what all the philosophers considered them - ignoramuses full of folly, stuck in their Kabbalah, who never tried their intellect to walk the paths of demonstrative wisdom to know a matter clearly, and who placed themselves in the blindness of faith that is of no benefit. But now I see that it is not so, and I truthfully admit that the Kabbalah is a true wisdom, and it is actual wisdom. On the contrary - it alone is the wisdom that informs of a matter correctly, more than all that is considered wisdom by all other people. I have already stood in my understanding and certainly seen that the true knowledge cannot be grasped by intellectual proofs, for it is only a kindness that the Lord has done to reveal this Kabbalah to Israel His people, that He passed it to them, and through it the intellect can truly delight and be satiated in its nature and desire to grasp and understand.

However, we have not yet come to the resolution of the first two difficulties I posed. First - how can corporeality develop from the sefirot? Second - how can we say that the Other Side, even its root, was mixed within the sefirot?

How Did Separate Beings and Matter Emerge from the Sefirot? Kabbalist: You have already seen that the very essence of this wisdom is the discernment of the root of all things, each thing on its own - what its matter is, where it emerged from and where it is going, meaning for what purpose and what benefit there is in it. Therefore, one who mixes the matters together is doing the very opposite of what is desired in wisdom, and will not attain it. In any case, we must speak of two things; if you do not distinguish between them, you will understand nothing but confusion:

The Divinity, blessed be He, meaning the Creator - not His essence, of which it is impossible to speak, but His will. And not even His will in terms of omnipotence, but in terms of ordered thought, meaning according to the things He wanted to establish in the creation of His world, all in proper order and gradation. This is one matter - the powers and attributes of the supreme will, according to which is the creation and the governance of the creatures.

The separate beings, meaning the created beings that are separate from the Creator. They are therefore not the Creator, nor His powers, nor His Divinity, but rather what He created with His power. If you mix these two matters, you will no longer understand any truth.

All matters of governance and the entire lawful order that the supreme will arranged to create the creatures with and guide them - this is the entire matter of the sefirot in all their conditions and their matters mentioned in them, which are included in ten sefirot, in five Partsufim. They are the totality of the powers of the supreme will, meaning its attributes in all their aspects according to what they are, in all their connections, how they are bound to each other and dependent on each other, such as compassion from kindness and dominion from judgment, and the totality of all the powers that He wanted to create with, and the totality of the order that He wanted with them, and the relation and connection that He wanted between them - this is the entirety of what is mentioned regarding the sefirot.

For all these matters are included in the ten sefirot and five Partsufim, and here the gradation of these powers in their proper order is known. The totality of the separate beings from their beginning to their end in their gradation is another matter. The truth is that the supreme Creator, blessed be He, created the separate beings specifically from nothing, and we cannot speak of the way He brought them out from nothingness into somethingness, for only He knows it.

Now we have here two subjects to investigate, each one as it is. A third matter is born to us from the existence of these two, which is the relation between them - between the sefirot and the separate beings. For even though we do not know the way of bringing out from nothing to something, we certainly know that the sefirot are what bring them out, and we know that each power brings out an offspring of its own that relates to it. Accordingly, we can understand many conditions in one power before it reaches the point of bringing out one offspring, and also a chain, meaning that one power extends from one power, a third power from the second, and so on with several powers. The last power will bring out one of the separate beings. The separate being was certainly rooted like a caused in its cause, even in the first of all the powers, and emerged only from the last one. These matters are simple to one who knows the laws of the prior and the subsequent, the cause and the caused. The main thing is to discern each thing in its proper context.

It turns out that when we see an investigation of the investigations of the wisdom, we must first discern what it is speaking about - whether the Divinity, blessed be He, or His creations, or the relation between the two. We will then immediately understand the matters according to the subject being spoken of. For what is spoken regarding the Divinity is nothing but the gradation of powers for the sake of maintaining the proper order according to a proper, conventional order. There, they do not speak of the differentiation of essences and their change, but rather of the order of powers and attributes - they are the lights I mentioned, which are parts of the will, blessed be He, which we have called light, as we explained above. What is spoken regarding the separate beings - there, there will be an actual change of essences, and their essential change in gradation. Meaning, there are the most subtle and great powers, such as what they called the soul and spirit of the chambers, and there are coarser ones, and they descend in gradation until they become these lower physical things. This is the light of the angels and the light of the Throne that our Sages, of blessed memory, explained was created first. From this light, all other creatures were created. When speaking of the relation between them, it is in terms of what we said - that each power brings out offspring that relate to it.

Just as all matters of the powers of will were included in ten sefirot, so too the matters of the separate beings were included in ten sefirot, and all their other distinctions. When we discern the worlds according to all the matters included in them, we say, as we explained above, that they are built of soul, spirit, soul, and all the other levels discerned in them, meaning garments and chambers and all that is mentioned about them in the investigations. Each of these matters is included in ten sefirot. Meaning, just as there are ten sefirot in the worlds of Divinity, so there are also ten sefirot in the Divinity, blessed be He, that spreads there to oversee His creatures. The creatures are in several ranks, this one higher than that. The closer to the matter of the Divinity, blessed be He, is the soul, and for those of the separate beings closer - spirit, and for those further - soul, and for those further - body, and for those further - garment, and for those further - chamber. In each of these levels, there are several divisions of things according to the matter of that level, each one as it is. All the matters in all the levels are always included in ten sefirot, and all that is mentioned in the order of the sefirot. From now on, it is up to the listener to discern in the investigations he hears - which sefirot it is speaking of, whether the soul, the spirit, or all the other aspects. The investigations proceed well according to the level they are expounded upon, not otherwise.

I will now come to the root of your questions. Your first question - that it seems the sefirot develop until they produce physicality, and you found it difficult that Divinity would develop and become a body. Here is the answer: We only say this in a place where it can be said, which is in the sefirot of the spirit and onward, in the worlds of Beriah, Yetzirah, Asiyah. But the spirit itself develops from the soul only in the way of something from nothing, nothing more. Nevertheless, the power that brings out this spirit has already been arranged in the conventions of gradation, so that it is found to relate in its value and matter to the spirit emerging from it. But the way of emergence is something from nothing. However, from the spirit onward, where all is separate, there is an actual, tangible development of something from something.

The Root of the Other Side in the Sefirot

Your second question was about the matter of the Other Side, whose root was within the sefirot. This too, when you examine it closely, you must discern where it is said, and then you will understand it according to the place it is said. This matter is first in the sefirot before there are created beings. If so, we are not speaking there of differentiated essences, but of the order of powers that will be arranged in one order, and then in another order, because of the matter desired in them. Since the supreme thought wants to think in the manner of human thought, even though it could have acted according to its omnipotence, it nevertheless acted only in the way of humans. When a person thinks to do something in its completeness, he must envision in his mind the good ways to do it, and those that are not good.

How does he discern these from those? Only if he envisions each thing in his thought as if it is done, and he sees the outcome that will come until the end of that matter. He will see the outcome from that matter, and he will either reject that matter from his will, or choose for himself another way. Therefore, the Holy One, blessed be He, wanted to show the two ways - what would be good to create the world with, and what would not be good. His powers were first arranged in one order, and no creature emerged from them, for He did not bring out creation in that order, but rather left those powers to make all their orders and all that depends on them. Now, what would emerge from them would be only great corruptions, kinds of evil things that would emerge and be born from them in the world if they were the ones acting and making the creation. Therefore, creation was not made from them, but from the arrangement of other powers. What we mean by the root of the Other Side is nothing but those powers that engender it, not an essence that is destined to be the Other Side in any way at all, for separate essences had not yet been created.

Now, I have answered you only so that you may know the style of the wisdom, but I cannot explain to you the reason for this entire matter and all its conditions, for you lack many premises that are needed prior to this. I have already told you: You do not know the matter of the kav (line) and reshimu (impression), the matter of Adam Kadmon, the lights of the ear, nose, mouth, and all the things you read whose matter you certainly do not know. The matter of the breaking comes after all these. When you know all these matters clearly, then I can tell you about the breaking, and you will see that I am telling you very long and profound matters. But now I only wanted to remove from the world the great difficulties which you found astonishing and with which you shook the entire world, just as all the other philosophers like you shake it.

The Descriptions of the Sefirot are Not Mere Metaphor

Philosopher: I have already left all these philosophers. I have seen, and I have already admitted, that the wisdom of Kabbalah has a very great advantage over all other wisdoms. However, I still have a great difficulty with the existence of most of the investigations expounded in this wisdom, for they embody matters in a very corporeal way. From this I find it difficult: If the matters are understood according to their plain meaning - this is impossible, for when speaking of the powers of the supreme will, it is inappropriate to speak of physical matters, for there is certainly no bodily semblance in the Creator, blessed be He, and this is a fundamental of faith. If you say they are metaphors, all the investigations are found to be metaphor and allegory, and none of them are matters as they are. Why then do we toil in vain with metaphors?

Kabbalist: They are certainly not metaphors, for all the sages would not have exerted themselves to use so many metaphors.

Philosopher: "For you saw no manner of form" (Deuteronomy 4:15) - how do you interpret this?

Kabbalist: This is certainly a great principle in the wisdom. That is why they said: From the mouths of scribes and not from books (Gittin 60b), for the sages themselves conceal the roots of the wisdom, to pass them on to whomever they deem fit. One who takes the text without knowing what is hidden in the heart of the author errs greatly on the path. Furthermore, it is impossible to write words that will suffice to give a correct understanding to every reader, just as eyeglasses cannot suit every eye. So too, there are no words that will suffice for all hearts and minds.

I will now come to answer your question. It is a full verse: "I have also spoken by the prophets, and I have multiplied visions" (Hosea 12:11). Tell me, how do you interpret this?

Philosopher: What interpretation is needed? Prophecy is a revelation that the Holy One, blessed be He, wants to reveal to the prophet, either matters of knowledge of His greatness, blessed be He, or future events that will come to the world. The supreme glory appears to the eyes of the prophet and shows him these matters. But it is the way of prophecy not to show the supreme glory or the things seen in a plain manner, but rather through imagery and visions. Meaning, the soul of the prophet imagines matters before it, like the matter of Ezekiel's chariot, and all other prophecies. Those images are the very knowledge that reaches the soul of the prophet, for even though he sees an image, he understands true knowledge.

Kabbalist: You have already resolved your difficulty. You have agreed that the prophets see the supreme glory in an imaginative way. All these matters are already explained in Scripture: "The Ancient of Days sat" (Daniel 7:9), "the likeness as the appearance of a man" (Ezekiel 1:26), and others like these. I too tell you that the entirety of the vision of the supreme glory according to the prophetic imagination is the entire tree of the sefirot and the Partsufim, and what the prophets abbreviated, the sages explained. The prophet to whom the Holy One, blessed be He, shows His chariot will see all that is mentioned in the words of Rabbi Shimon bar Yochai, of blessed memory, and his commentators, and all that is mentioned in the chapters of the chambers, and all similar to them. Therefore, the investigations of this wisdom are not metaphors, for they are true, and they are the entirety of what the prophets see when they behold the supreme glory and His chariots. But this we know, that all the prophets see is in an imaginative way, and they themselves know the truth in this, which is: "To whom then will you liken Me, that I should be equal to him?" (Isaiah 40:25). However, the benefit of knowing all these prophetic visions is the very benefit that reaches the prophets themselves when they see it, for these visions are what inform all the orders of governance and its laws to the prophets who see, and to the sages who know in their tradition what the prophets see.

Philosopher: This matter settles in my heart, and I desire to learn this wisdom in a proper manner, for I see in it a very great and upright profundity. However, I did not understand the words of the texts and became greatly confused by them. Now I am divesting myself of all I knew and read of this, and I ask of you to favor me to teach me in a properly direct manner from the very beginning of the entire matter as is fitting, if you desire to benefit me.

Regarding this matter of vision, I still have questions: What do the prophets see in their visions? For it is written: "For you saw no manner of form" (Deuteronomy 4:15). Even the verses themselves contradict each other, for in one place it says: "And he beholds the form of the Lord" (Numbers 12:8). Also, I desire to know the matter which I saw the sages of the Kabbalah greatly perplexed by, which is the matter of the state of the worlds. In one place it seems that Asiyah is in the center of the worlds and the kav pierces and penetrates within it down to the end of the circles of Atik, while in another place it seems that it is beneath the feet of Adam Kadmon and in his heels, and I did not see a satisfactory answer. But I do not want you to answer me each matter on its own, for I have already seen that a different kind of study is needed for the wisdom. Therefore, I beseech you to guide me on a straight path from beginning to end.

Kabbalist: I will do so, and I will teach you a teaching sufficient for a wise man like yourself, to descend to the end of this matter upon which the wisdom is built. I will now tell you what order is needed to study this wisdom. You have heard that there is the entirety of the visions seen in the chariot, and afterward the matters of governance desired in these visions. One must first know the entire vision, and afterward the interpretation.

Philosopher: I am pleased that you are proceeding with me in order, for it is a great principle that without order there is nothing but confusion, and it is impossible to learn anything. For the intellect cannot settle on a matter that is stuffed into it perplexed and confused, unless it sees its parts, each thing upon its wheels, and all its matters - each flock on its own, until each matter is clarified in its place.

The Main Point of the Wisdom - To Know the Way of Governance

Kabbalist: See that this matter is certainly true, that to know only the names of the sefirot and Partsufim and all that is found in them, without knowing their nature and purpose, is not knowledge at all. For what benefit is there to know that there are several kinds of lights above to guide the world, if we do not know what governance extends from them to these creatures guided by them? What do we see of the profundity of His wisdom, blessed be He, in this matter, and His deep counsel? But if we can truly grasp the secret of His counsel, blessed be He, in the creation of His world and the way of His governance, until all the things that were found and done are well understood, all with good reason and knowledge, with a wondrous profundity of thought that knew to cause things to orbit in such an exalted orbit, that all these outcomes emerged from there, and all is proper and rectified - this is what we call wisdom. If we find the entire essence of this governance, which is nothing but these sefirot and all their laws, then when we speak of the sefirot and what is in them, we will no longer say that we are speaking of a narrative of things that are like the words of a sealed book, but rather of one great wisdom, which is the wisdom of knowing His exalted governance, blessed be He, to the extent that we are given to grasp and know.

Philosopher: There is certainly no doubt about this, for that is why I could not bear the things I would hear about this wisdom, because I saw them as unseasoned bread, and I did not find in them any rectified matter of wisdom. But in this generation, on the contrary, I say that it is a very wondrous wisdom, and it is certainly fitting for any person of knowledge to set aside all other kinds of wisdom in the world for the sake of this great and holy wisdom, for all other wisdoms are nothing compared to this great wisdom.

Kabbalist: From now on, we need to learn two things in order, one after the other, as I told you: First, one must know the entirety of all that we have in our tradition - what is in the vision of the supernal chariot, meaning the entirety of the sefirot and all the laws mentioned in them, for this matter stands only in tradition, as it was passed down to us by the masters of prophecy and the holy spirit. Afterward, one must review all this and know the interpretation of this entire vision. The entirety of this interpretation is the entirety of the supernal governance, according to what we are given to grasp, as we said above. Therefore, I will divide all this into two parts:

The first - I will arrange for you the entirety of the holy tree, and all that is in it, in short chapters, so that you can accustom yourself to always know them, that they should be sharp in your mouth. For one who wants to understand the investigations of the wisdom, which wander here and there in the chapters of the tree and its branches, must always know all of these.

Afterward, I will arrange for you the entirety of the interpretation, meaning the entirety of the supernal governance in its conventions. On this too, I will arrange for you premises in short definitions to come to the nature of this knowledge, with which you can then properly walk in the paths of wisdom and its ways.

Part Two

In the Ten Chapters of the Entirety of the Tree, the Roots of the Wisdom of Truth are Included

Philosopher: I am here, my brother, with all the desire of my soul, to receive from you what you have promised me, for I cannot restrain myself from ascending in the sweetness of your wisdom, which my soul has yearned for and pined after your pleasant words, and for the holiness of this wondrous wisdom, to which my eyes have been opened to see, and I saw what I had not considered nor had it entered my heart. Now, favor me please with your good promise.

Kabbalist: I have done as you said, and here are the short chapters I have arranged, to be fluent in your mouth.

Philosopher: I have already heard that you want to include in these chapters all that is in the sefirot and the supernal worlds, according to the tradition of the masters of the holy spirit. Nevertheless, I would like to know from you - did you gather in them all that is found written in the words of the Kabbalists, or what did you take and place in them?

Kabbalist: If I wanted to take all that the holy Rabbi Isaac Luria, of blessed memory, said, I would have lengthened greatly and not established them upon clear knowledge, for the burden would be too great for you, and you would see no end to the matters. But this is simple, that every wisdom has roots and branches, and I took the root and left the branches. For once you know the roots, you will understand all the branches that depend on them when you find them in the words of the Kabbalists. But if I were to omit one of the roots, afterward, when you would find one investigation built upon it, you would not understand it at all.

Roots and Branches in the Wisdom of Truth

Philosopher: The matter is good, and I hope to receive much knowledge from you, because you clarify the way of study greatly. But please inform me, what do you call a root, and what branches in this wisdom?

Kabbalist: I call a root that which is one subject in the wisdom, and a branch - what is expounded upon the known subjects. We must know all the subjects accepted by the masters of the holy spirit, them and their names, their states, and all that depends on their structure. The entirety of all this I call the holy tree. To this I call roots, because upon each one of these, many investigations then emerge. If we do not know the subject, the investigation is not understood at all. But when we know this, what is expounded in each of them is great, and there is also no end to all the great details expounded upon that subject, and I have no need to gather them, for when you know all the roots, you will know all the details on your own when you read them in their place. I will tell you more clearly this matter: All our engagement is with the powers of will decreed from the will itself, for all creation and its governance to be according to them, and they are all the laws of this creation, this governance, and their conventions. Now, the intellect must recognize that each deed will not need its own law, and that there will not be as many laws as there are deeds. Rather, it is of wisdom to establish one way and one law that can suffice for every deed that will be born after this, at every time that will be.

Philosopher: This is simple to me, for multiplicity where paucity suffices is a deficiency. On the contrary, the perfection of the Emanator, blessed be His name, is that He gave this matter, that He will not need separate laws for the fundamentals, but rather, that He will envision unified visions and establish one way sufficient for all.

Kabbalist: But this general law is the matter of the ten sefirot, to which there is nothing to add and from which there is nothing to subtract. These suffice for every time and every occurrence, due to the great number of conditions found in their completeness, for He who envisions everything envisioned all that is needed, and gathered and included everything in these ten, so that no new existence will be needed after the first existence. However, the ways in which all things will be born from the ten sefirot in their times - these too were established from the beginning according to what is needed for all. But the outcomes themselves that emerge from them - they are all the creatures and the occurrences that were born afterward, according to the ways already prepared in them. Now, the entirety of all these ways is what there is to know, for all the changes that changed afterward and that change in all of existence depend on them. If we subtract from our knowledge one of these ways, we will subtract from our knowledge several creatures that emerge from there, for it is impossible to know how they emerge. These are the ways of what I included for you in these chapters, they are the entirety of the ways I call the holy tree.

The Kabbalah of the Ramak and of the Arizal

Philosopher: Please inform me of one thing I yearn to know, which is the matter of the two Kabbalot that exist - the Kabbalah of Ramak, of blessed memory, and the Kabbalah of the Arizal, of blessed memory. What are they, and what is the difference between them?

Kabbalist: They are both certainly true, and there is no dispute between them. Rather, I have already explained to you in my words both of them. I already told you that the ten sefirot are the first foundation sufficient for all governance. Thus, any occurrence that occurs in the world will certainly be born from the movement of one of these sefirot. It is possible for us to know the sefirah from which it will be born, but not the specific way fixed in it to give birth to that matter. Our knowledge may be more profound, and we may also know the specific way of that sefirah, in which it gave birth to that occurrence. These are the two Kabbalot of the Ramak and the Arizal:
The Ramak, of blessed memory, only explained the ten sefirot and all that is born from them, but not the way how they give birth to things. All that he said is true, and the entire Torah can

be interpreted in this way, for in truth, everything emerges from these. However, the Arizal, of blessed memory, explained to us a clearer knowledge, for he explained the specific ways of the sefirot, and through them we know how different things emerge from one sefirah, for each one has its own way.

This is the relation and connection between sefirah and sefirah, for according to these connections is the emergence of their offspring according to their matters. But the changes that change through these ways are without number, and they are those that I called the branches of the root, for outside of these mentioned ways, no investigation will be found that speaks of them at all.

Philosopher: Can you tell me in brief all these subjects?

Kabbalist: They are all the worlds from after the tzimtzum until the end of Asiyah, and their entirety - Adam Kadmon with all its known branches, Atzilut in its five Partsufim, with all their parts and the values of their arrangements, their fixed and changing states, all these fixed and changing matters - in what it is fixed and in what it changes. The entirety of all this is the root of the wisdom, and the rest is its interpretation. Now pay attention and understand, for the branches have no end, and the details have no limit. Once you have grasped the root, you will receive of the details as God grants you.

Philosopher: Speak your words, for I am listening to you with all my heart and all my soul.

Kabbalist: Here are the ten chapters, I have arranged them in a concise way. Hear them, and know them.

Philosopher: I have already heard and seen your chapters, and your words are good and correct. They are the roots of the wisdom that one must know, all of them fluent in the mouth, to then hear in the studies the details of the matters. Now let me hear from you the interpretation of all this, for the matter appears to the eyes that the matters go to a much greater depth. It is not acceptable to the intellect that they do not have a deeper intention, for if not, they would all be like a sealed book, and there are many difficulties with them. It is impossible to understand them except with a great explanation.

Kabbalist: As you have spoken, so I will do, and I will give you the interpretation of all this with God's help. But I want to hear from you, what is it that you find so difficult in these matters, after you have heard what I have already explained to you.

Philosopher: I will do as you have spoken. But let us make of this another debate, for I see that the matters are very long. We are also moving on to another matter, for until now we have done "a man must always learn," and afterward we will fulfill "and afterward he may delve into it and analyze it" (Shabbat 63a).

Part Three

Kabbalist: Here I am, my brother. Arrange your words and I will hear them.

Complete Understanding in the Wisdom of Truth is Understanding the Ways of Governance

Philosopher: You have already prefaced me with one necessary premise from natural intellect, that one who wishes to know this wisdom must certainly know all the matters of the sefirot and Partsufim - their nature and actions, for if not, he will not be called one who knows this wisdom, but one who remembers the names mentioned in this wisdom. For when a person knows that there are so many Partsufim, so many states, so many ascents, so many descents, and all the other matters mentioned in the wisdom, but does not know where they are heading and to what point all these lines are drawn - what knowledge does he have? He has nothing but a jumble of many matters in his head, like "a basket full of books" (Megillah 28b).

So, even if we leave the first difficulty that ostensibly appears on the face of the entire wisdom, namely the embodiment, that these investigations in their superficiality greatly embody the divine matters, which is against the true faith, and we have already left this when we generally knew that all this is nothing but the vision of prophecy, but all that is seen is nothing but attributes and laws of the Divinity, blessed be He, in how He sustains and governs His creatures - at first we still desire to specify and know how all this is the order of conventions and governance. Furthermore, the matters have no order at all, neither beginning nor end, and we find the investigations leaping from one matter to another, without any connection.

Kabbalist: Explain your words. Where did you find the lack of order that you speak of?

Questions on the Order of Tzimtzum and Worlds

Philosopher: I also heard this from the outside, for you did not bring it in your words. But it is written in the words of Rabbi Chaim Vital, of blessed memory, that in the empty space remaining from the tzimtzum there are infinite worlds, but they only speak of one detail. This is difficult for me either way - either the rest of these worlds have effects in creation and governance or not. If you say no, then they were in vain. If you say they have an effect, then when one detail is known - what have we gained? It is not even a drop in the sea compared to the infinite worlds. It cannot be said that from this detail the world emerges, and from the rest of the worlds - other matters that are not in this world. For if we say this, we will no longer find our hands and feet in all this wisdom. Was not the tzimtzum and all of Atzilut only for the sake of this world? Who knows of other worlds besides the chain of Atzilut, Beriah, Yetzirah, and Asiyah? If so, what are they and why are they?

Kabbalist: All this is regarding what I did not say. State your difficulties with what I did say.

On the Order of the Branches of Adam Kadmon

Philosopher: When you came to detail this alone, you began and said that it contains AB, SAG, MA, and BaN. It seems you wanted to arrange the order of the emanation of these Names' branches. If you had done so, I would have known at least one thing. But AB you left outside, and you began with SAG, dividing it into AB, SAG, MA, BaN. I thought you would arrange their order, but you did not do this either. Rather, you divided AB of SAG into three reasons: upper, middle, lower, each a group of lights on its own.

I also thought the Nekudot (points) would be similarly divided, but you did not divide them so. Instead, you included them all together. Then you skipped from this to MA, and there too you did not divide at all, but included everything together. Matters also became confused in my ears between BaN of SAG and the general BaN.

In sum, I am perplexed by your many words, which are all good in themselves, but I do not find any order that flows entirely from the beginning of the matters to their end, which is what I would desire to hear.

Kabbalist: Until now you have judgment and reason, each individually. I will explain it to you with God's help. If you have further confusions, complete your words.

Regarding the Lights of Ear, Nose, Mouth

Philosopher: You spoke of the Lights of Ear, Nose, Mouth, and I do not know what they are or their matter. For according to what I heard from you, the creatures of this world do not come from them at all. What is even more difficult for me is the matter of the Lights of the Mouth, in which the act of emanation and return is mentioned, and I do not know what these matters are or their purpose.

If you say we cannot know the thoughts of the Emanator, blessed be He, then why do we need to know anything at all about these matters? I am very confused by your words, which are all good in themselves, but I do not find any order that flows from the beginning of the matters to their end, which is what I would desire to hear.

The letters mentioned in the Lights of Ear, Nose, Mouth - in the Ear, Heh; in the Nose, Vav; in the Mouth, Dalet Yod - there must be some matter to these letters. In sum, all this is surely only a superficial version, and I do not know in them any reason that would settle the heart to see in it wisdom and knowledge.

I see in the Lights of the Mouth one incident, namely emanation and return. In the Nekudot, another incident, namely the shattering. Surely there must be a reason and root for all this. I know that explanations will not be lacking to resolve each matter on its own, but I will not believe that these matters are so separate, that each one is a wisdom on its own.

Rather, I believe there is one general order, arranging all these matters together. The explanations that will be found in it to detail according to this general order - these I will accept, and know that I have stood upon the clarity of matters.

Regarding the Shattering

See, the matter of the shattering contains so many matters that I do not know how to enter into them:

That the vessels were one underneath the other and not corresponding to each other; that the lights entered and returned backwards. For all this, there must be a great root and sufficient reason.

I also have a great difficulty with the words of the Arizal regarding the shattering, even though I saw that you endeavored to resolve it, but I desire to properly understand the matter. For they said that the sefirot of Atzilut were shattered and descended to BYA - the inner part to Beriah, the middle to Yetzirah, and the outer to Asiyah. But afterwards, they all returned and ascended, and made Atzilut.

If so, from where did BYA emerge? One cannot say they are a new illumination that emerged from the first, for it is stated regarding the clarification that the good remained in Atzilut and the lesser descended to BYA. Now Atzilut is greatly lacking.

Regarding the matter of the 288 sparks, the Arizal makes many calculations to arrive at the number 288. This is very difficult for me - why do we need this calculation? If it was a straightforward calculation, that reality was so, fine. But why do we need to seek so many reasons to arrive at this number? Either count all that descended or do not count any number at all.

Regarding the clarification, they said that the end of Malchut of Asiyah was not clarified, to the point that the Arizal stated it is forbidden to draw from Malchut of Asiyah; rather, one must draw from Malchut of Yetzirah. These words have no explanation at all. What does it mean to draw from Malchut of Asiyah or from Malchut of Yetzirah? The awe is one - to fear the Master of all. How do we understand this division - to fear from one sefirah or another?

Regarding the tikun (repair), there too are so many scattered paths and matters that there is no knowledge to gather them.

Kabbalist: Such as what?

Regarding the Repairs

Philosopher: Such as Reisha D'lo Ityada (the head that is not known) and the doubts mentioned in it. I have two difficulties with this:
First, what need is there for these doubts and to know them? Furthermore, these doubts exist in all of Atzilut. If so, they should all be called "Lo Ityada" (not known).

Regarding Arich Anpin, they said it has three heads. What is the relevance of this matter? Let us say it has Keter, Chochmah and Da'at, like all the others. There must be a great root to this matter, that it is mentioned as a very great secret.

So too, all the other repairs: the seven Tikunim of the head, the thirteen Tikunim of the beard. How could there be so many lights without action? This is impossible! These matters require a great explanation.

Abba, Imma, Yisrael Saba and Tevunah - there are so many types of divisions in them. In Ze'ir Anpin and Nukvah, in their smallness and greatness and unions, there are so many types of matters. What does it mean, first and second smallness and greatness?

If we resolve with one general answer that all this is the chain in order to arrive at this world, let us say in one general statement: We do not know anything. Rather, answer that there are many levels in order to arrive at this world. And as we skipped all the other worlds in the vacuum, so too let us skip all these matters.

Kabbalist: I have heard your difficulties. Behold, I am arranging for you 138 short orders, bordering the entirety of the governance over all the matters of the Tree in an extremely concise way. You must pay attention to every word and see wisdom abundant and profound. Here it is before you:

Opening 1: The unity of the Infinite, blessed be He... etc. until Opening 138.

Part Four

The Way of Study of the Book "138 Openings of Wisdom"

Philosopher: I have seen the depth of the wisdom and the borders that you have bordered concisely. They are very fitting to receive complete knowledge of these matters, containing the abundant in little. However, one who does not descend to the depth of the matters passes over them quickly and does not pause to understand each part individually.

They already said: Everything is easy for one who does not understand. Therefore, I will ask of you to favor me, and after you have abridged the lengthy, lengthen the concise. Show me regarding the concise statements how many propositions are included in them, and to how many aspects one needs to turn in that matter in order to grasp it from all its sides.

Therefore, divide each and every statement into parts and discernments. Then I will be compelled to understand it, contemplate each part, and I will not pass over. Thus I will properly enter the chambers of this wisdom, for the matters will be expansive before me. After that, the grasp - to grasp this profound subject. Indeed, kindness belongs to God, for "God grants wisdom from His mouth, knowledge and understanding" (Proverbs 2:6).

Kabbalist: I will do as you say, for it is my desire to lead you in the good way, to properly stand upon the content of this wisdom. Here is the explanation of the 138 borders that I have arranged for you:

The foundation of wisdom and the pillar of faith, etc. until the end.

Part Five

Philosopher: I have heard from you wisdom abundant and profound, and it is upon me now to write it upon the tablet of my heart, to contemplate it constantly day by day, for I know that all my days will not suffice to reach the end of this great wisdom. This is the root of what I have received from you. Now, please inform me, based on this root, to how many aspects will the matters of this wisdom turn? For I already think that if we know this too, we will know where to turn after knowing this root.

Four Areas of Knowledge in the Wisdom of Truth

Kabbalist: There are four areas of knowledge in the Wisdom, as explained by the holy Rabbi Shimon bar Yochai, may his memory be for a blessing, in the Zohar Chadash on Shir HaShirim, on the verse: "If you do not know" (Song of Songs 1:8), he said: The wisdom that a person needs to contemplate, etc.

Philosopher: It would give me pleasure to hear this matter properly, for now you know that I will stand on the path of wisdom, to know how to properly use the root for all the details.

The Chain of Emanation of the Worlds

Kabbalist: These are the four areas of knowledge: The first is the knowledge of the emanation of the Supreme Light, which created the worlds and governs them, and this is called "to contemplate the secret of his Master," which is what we grasp about the Creator, may He be blessed. And this is the first area of knowledge that I have conveyed to you thus far, which is the knowledge of the Tree in all its details and governance. This is called the knowledge of the emanation of the Supreme Light, for in all this, the Light that was emanated after the Contraction spreads out, and this is all that there is to it. The totality of this includes: the Contraction of the Infinite, blessed be He, the Impression that remains, the Line that enters, Adam Kadmon and its branches, which are: the Lights of the Skull, Ear-Nose-Mouth, and the Lights of the Mouth which are the Akudim, the matter of the emergence of the Vessel through the emergence of the Sefirot and their return, and the Lights of the Eyes which are the Nekudim, their shattering and fall, the World of Tikun in all its Partsufim, namely: Atik, Arich Anpin, Abba and Imma, Zeir Anpin and its Nukva, the other Illuminations in Atzilut, namely: Yisrael Saba and Tevuna, Jacob and Leah, and the other inscribed Illuminations, namely: the Tribes, the Generation of the Desert, and the other diagonals. And all these - to know the state of all these Partsufim and their enclothements, their smallness, their greatness, their ascents, their unifications, Mayin Duchrin, Mayin Nukvin; and after that the matters of Beriah, Yetzirah, Asiyah, the Heichalot within them, and the Divinity that spreads within them in the secret of the Glory that descends into Beriah; and likewise what appears to correspond to His blessed holiness and oppose it, to make room for the deeds of the lower beings, namely: the Other Side and its Sefirot and all its parts. This is the entirety of this area of knowledge.

The Connection and Relationship of Man and Creatures with the Worlds

The second area of knowledge delves into the nature of man and the secret of his divine image. It explores the connection between man and all the worlds, the impact he has on them, and their influence on him. This area covers man's arrival in this world, his departure from it, and everything that pertains to his existence. It provides a deeper understanding of the Sefirot and the actions of their Lights, which correspond precisely to the image of man and the laws and decrees of his nature. The laws of divine providence and the emergence of creatures from the Sefirot are also dependent on this area. It examines how creatures are born, their essence, and the cycles they undergo from the beginning of their existence until the completion of their rectification, each according to its unique nature.

The third area of knowledge involves contemplating the secrets of souls and their reincarnations. It encompasses the many intricate matters found within this realm. There are two levels of knowledge here: the superficial level, which involves understanding the laws of reincarnation in all its details, and the inner level, which explores how the clarification of divine providence and the completion of the illumination of the Malchut (Kingdom) given to the service of lower beings is entirely dependent on souls. The ways of clarification are the ways of reincarnation mentioned earlier. All the deeds performed under the heavens, from the beginning of creation until the end of the six thousand years, depend on this process. It is through reincarnation that the world will eventually reach a state of rest, when divine providence will have been fully clarified, and there will be no further need for rectification.

The fourth area of knowledge involves contemplating the secret of this world and understanding how all its creatures are governed. It goes beyond the superficial understanding of creatures and the ways of nature that philosophers have observed, recognizing that their perspective is limited and does not represent the complete truth. This area delves into the true essence of all creatures and their inner workings.

All creatures are governed according to one inner governance, and the internality that enclothes all creatures, which is what they said: "Nature" is the same numerical value as "Elokim". And this is the truth that the Holy One, blessed be He, hid from the philosophers. And this knowledge was given only to the sages of Israel, and most of the midrashim of our Sages, which speak of the work of creation and the matters of all the generations of heaven and earth, revolve around the axis of this main and inner governance.

Therefore, they differ from the ways of the philosophers. And there are things that seem strange, and that the senses testify to the contrary. But the truth is, they are speaking according to the true governance that is hidden from the eyes of men, and it is passed down to them from the prophets and from the holy spirit. Now, this knowledge is divided into two, namely: knowledge of this governance below, how the lower creatures are governed according to the influence of the Sefirot, and the command of the appointed ones over each creature; and there is also knowledge of what is in the Sefirot themselves, corresponding to these things below, and for the purpose of these things below. For everything that exists below, besides being governed by the higher ones, also has its counterpart above. And these are the four areas of knowledge that come after the root that I have explained to you, and their matters are found in the treasuries of our Sages and the specialties of Rabbi Shimon bar Yochai, may his memory be for a blessing, the holy one of Israel. And you are wise, understand as the goodness of your intellect, and God will help you, for "the Lord gives wisdom; from His mouth come knowledge and understanding" (Proverbs 2:6).

There is a need to make a short order for beginners

Philosopher: Behold, all that you have said is very good, and I think it is enough to know the root of wisdom thoroughly. And there is a way in my heart that I am going and contemplating, that it would be possible to do to expand the way of this wisdom, for not all intellects are equal, and the opinions of people differ greatly from one another, and it is necessary to expand the way not only for one intellect, but for all, if possible.

Kabbalist: Please tell your advice, for I know you are a man of order, and I also agree with your words and your divisions, for they are certainly beneficial to repair the paths in the soul, to straighten them and widen them. One who studies without order - it is impossible to receive wisdom, for the studies become mixed up in his mind, and nothing remains in its proper place.

Philosopher: What was needed - is to make a short order for the beginner in this wisdom to start with, so that he can run in its ways without stumbling. And I will tell you my reasons. Behold, a very proper order of study is to teach the chapters that you have arranged at first, and then the 138 Openings of Wisdom, and then their explanation. This is true, and it is what a person needs to reach the proper knowledge. But there is an intellect that will not be able to contain all the chapters at first, before knowing anything about the governance, for the matters are strange in his eyes, and he does not descend into their depth at all. And the matters are many, not few, that he can wait until the end, and if you want to make one understand the content of the matters, if he is not a patient man - he will not be able to wait so long without understanding.

Kabbalist: The matter is good, please tell how you want this order.

Philosopher: So, we shall do, I will tell you according to the order that I think is good - tell me this matter or that matter, and you will answer me with your Kabbalah.

Kabbalist: So, we shall do, begin to ask, and I will answer you about everything you want.

Philosopher: I will begin. Answer me this first: what is the need for this wisdom?

Kabbalist: All creatures are governed according to a single inner governance, an internality that enclothes all of creation. This is what our Sages referred to when they said: "Nature" has the same numerical value as "Elokim" (God). This is the truth that the Holy One, blessed be He, concealed from the philosophers.

This knowledge was given exclusively to the sages of Israel. Most of the midrashim of our Sages, which discuss the work of creation and the matters of all the generations of heaven and earth, revolve around the axis of this primary and inner governance. Consequently, they differ from the ways of the philosophers. Some things may seem strange and contradictory to our senses, but the truth is that the Sages are speaking according to the true governance hidden from the eyes of men, passed down to them from the prophets and the holy spirit. This knowledge is divided into two aspects: the governance below, how the lower creatures are governed according to the influence of the Sefirot and the command of the appointed ones over each creature; and the knowledge of what is in the Sefirot themselves, corresponding to these things below and serving their purpose.

Everything that exists below, besides being governed by the higher ones, also has its counterpart above. These are the four areas of knowledge that come after the root that I have explained to you, and their matters are found in the treasuries of our Sages and the specialties of Rabbi Shimon bar Yochai, may his memory be for a blessing, the holy one of Israel. You are wise, so understand according to the goodness of your intellect, and God will help you, for "the Lord gives wisdom; from His mouth come knowledge and understanding" (Proverbs 2:6).

Philosopher: I agree that the arrangement you have presented is very good and sufficient for thoroughly understanding the root of wisdom. However, I have been contemplating a way to expand the path of this wisdom, recognizing that not all intellects are equal and people's opinions differ greatly from one another. It is necessary to broaden the way not only for one intellect but for all, if possible.

Kabbalist: Your words and divisions are certainly beneficial for repairing the paths in the soul, straightening and widening them. Studying without order makes it impossible to receive wisdom, as the concepts become muddled in one's mind, and nothing remains in its proper place.

Philosopher: What is needed is a concise order for beginners to start with, enabling them to navigate the paths of this wisdom without stumbling. The proper order of study would be to first teach the chapters you have arranged, then the 138 Openings of Wisdom, followed by their explanation. This is the path a person should take to reach proper knowledge. However, some intellects may struggle to grasp all the chapters initially, before understanding anything about the governance, as the matters may seem strange and profound to them. The subject matter is extensive, and not everyone has the patience to wait until the end for understanding.

Kabbalist: Please explain how you envision this order.

Philosopher: I will tell you what I think is a good arrangement - pose a question on this matter or that matter, and you will answer me with your Kabbalah. Let us proceed in this manner; begin asking, and I will answer everything you wish to know.

Kabbalist: As we shall do, begin to ask, and I will answer you about everything you want.

Philosopher: To begin, please answer this first: what is the need for this wisdom?

The Wisdom of Truth explains the ways of Divine providence

Kabbalist: The need for this wisdom is great. And I will give you a few answers to this. First, I will tell you that we are obligated to know it, for it is a commandment upon us, as it is written: "And you shall know this day and take unto your heart that the Lord is God in the heavens above and on the earth below; there is none else" (Deuteronomy 4:39). Thus, we are obligated to know with knowledge, and not with faith alone, but with matters that settle upon the heart, as it explicitly states: "and take unto your heart." And what is it that we must know? The truth of His oneness, blessed be He: "For the Lord is God in the heavens above and on the earth below; there is none else," and so on. Therefore, there are two things we need to know: The first - that the Unique One is the One who oversees and governs everything, both the upper and lower worlds. And the second - that there is none besides Him. These two things that we need to know, you tell me: From where shall we know them, and what wisdom will make them known to us?

We need to know that the Holy One, blessed be He, governs everything, and to know this with clear knowledge in matters that settle upon the heart. We cannot understand this from the simple meaning of the Torah, for what does the simple meaning of the Torah revolve around? Only around the commandments, the manner of their performance and all their laws, or in understanding the stories of the deeds that occurred, as they are mentioned in it.

These are the two parts in the simple meaning of the Torah. From the first part, we will certainly not learn this, for the performance of the commandments and their laws do not inform us of His oneness, blessed be He, and His perfection at all, for all that learning could have been commandments from a person whom we would desire, or need, to serve, or to understand his words. If so, this knowledge does not emerge from here. If you say it emerges from the stories, it is obvious that it does not, for the stories are not judgments, but rather deeds and not knowledge.

If you say that by delving into those stories, this will emerge for you, then you need another analysis of the stories themselves, which will explain how those deeds were done according to the supreme providence with profound wisdom. This is a separate study in itself and is not the study of the stories in the Torah. And even if you want to derive from the wondrous stories themselves - that since these wonders were performed, it must be that the Holy One, blessed be He, oversees and acts - this is not called anything but you deducing in your mind that it must be so.

However, this does not mean that you know with wisdom and knowledge that it is so, and that you have grasped the entire governance of the world and understood its ways, to see with settled thought that it is all from the Unique One, blessed be He, with great wisdom, as it truly is. The intention of the commandment is "And you shall know this day and take unto your heart" - knowledge and settling of the heart, to know in a way of actual wisdom that the matter is so, that everything in the world is the governance of His blessed name, and that it is all good and properly arranged, not just in a way of faith, but in a way of knowledge, that you understand and comprehend that it is so good and proper. This you will certainly not be able to derive from the stories at all.

Furthermore, from the stories you will derive that at those times, the Holy One, blessed be He, acted in this way in His world, but not because of this will you derive that all natural governance - He governs. On the contrary, the heretic can say, God forbid: The miracles are from the Holy One, blessed be He, but the natural things are not from Him; rather, He lets things proceed by natural chance, and His providence does not act upon them. If you say to derive this knowledge of wisdom from the wisdom of nature, as others thought, to call the natural things "the work of creation" (see footnote 155), this is certainly not so, for even deniers of providence contemplate nature; on the contrary, they are the ones who say - the world proceeds according to its custom.

And if from all these you will not derive this knowledge, the commandment is still upon you to fulfill it. There is no way to fulfill it except through this Wisdom of Truth, for it is the one that reveals and informs of this true matter of providence, and all that depends on it, and it will inform of His oneness, blessed be He, in all the aspects that one can conceive. For its entire matter is only this - to make known the supreme oneness, blessed be He, properly, and to make known that everything that was, is, and will be - is all overseen by Him with individual providence, and to explain the ways of this providence, and to explain through them all the deeds, meaning - the creations in the world, and all the deeds that were done to them, from the first day until the end of everything.

Philosopher: Why should we toil with all this effort to see if you can find this knowledge from other places? I will bring you a clear proof for your words that leaves no doubt. See, the investigation establishes its own unique foundation for each subject, and the matters of that subject must be explained through that investigation alone, not any other. This is simple. There are now in existence the Creator, blessed be He, and His creatures. We thus have here two investigations: the investigation of the Creator, blessed be He, and the investigation of the creatures. Regarding the Creator, we cannot investigate His existence, for it is forbidden to us and utterly incomprehensible.

We can only investigate the relation between the Creator and His creatures, meaning the investigation of the Creator insofar as He oversees them to bestow upon them or to receive their service. Tell me now, the investigation of the Creator is not the investigation of the creatures, nor any other investigation, but only that which depends on the Creator, blessed be He, namely the relation between Him and His creations. One who wishes to know matters that depend on the relation between the Creator and the creatures, to which investigation shall he turn? He must go only to investigate the Divinity of the blessed One, which is the investigation we mentioned of the relation between the Creator and the creatures.

Let us now make a deduction: The Holy One, blessed be He, commands us to know His providence. We now wish to study what will inform us of this providence. What will inform us of this providence is none other than the wisdom of truth, for it is what reveals and informs the true matter of providence and all that depends on it. It will inform us of His unity, blessed be He, in all the aspects that can be conceived. For its entire matter is this alone - to properly convey the supreme unity and to convey that all that was, is, and will be is entirely guided by Him with individual providence, to explain the ways of this providence, and to explain through them all the deeds, meaning the creatures in the world and all the deeds done with them, from the first day until the very end. We thus see without a doubt that there is an obligation to study the wisdom of truth.

Kabbalist: Your words are good, and from your speech, the Supernal One shall be praised.

The Wisdom of Truth Explains That All is From God for Good, Even What Appears Evil

Philosopher: This you said as a first reason. You must complete your words.

Kabbalist: The second is that even if we were not commanded in this, we would need to pursue it in order to calm our thoughts and have our path clear before our eyes, to be saved from the evil inclination and its terrible confusion. See, what the evil inclination constantly places as a screen before our eyes is showing that the world proceeds in chaos and happenstance, as if there is no judgment and no Judge. King Solomon, peace be upon him, already gathered all the matters that circulate in the mouths of people in the book of Ecclesiastes. He begins there: "Vanity of vanities," and shows all the matters of this world and all the follies of people who stray far from the straight path, all because they do not know the truth clearly.

According to what is visible to the eyes, anyone who increases his efforts in commerce becomes wealthy, and one who has silver and gold is honored. We have seen thousands upon thousands that it is not so, but slaves riding on horses and princes walking like slaves. Those who grasp Torah are lowly and despised, while the nations of the world stand in tranquility. Israel is harried and storm-tossed in this swift, bitter exile; no one pays any mind, and they are in the nethermost level with no one awakening to repentance. The Torah is being forgotten. It is true that regarding all this it is said: "But the righteous shall live by his faith" (Habakkuk 2:4). However, if you find one wisdom that explains all these matters with a satisfactory explanation, clarifying everything properly and showing that all this is from God for good, and showing how this is so - in clear, orderly study - would it not be of great benefit for us to pursue it with all manner of pursuit?

Through the Wisdom of Truth, we Understand the Mitsvot and their Details

Third - the service that we perform for the Holy One, blessed be He. It is true that it is desirable not to seek reasons for the commandments, but rather to perform them as they said, with closed eyes. However, you will see that it is impossible for the intellects of people to stand firm in the details of commandments that seem to be matters that are not so significant. The Sages already said: "Matters that stand at the height of the world, yet people treat them lightly" (Berachot 6b).

Have not the heretics already breached and permitted regarding the words of the Sages, that if a gentile touched wine it becomes yayin nesech (libation wine)? "One who eats three meals on Shabbat is saved from the judgment of Gehinnom" (Shabbat 118a), and "One who recites Tehillah LeDavid (Psalms 145) every day is assured that he is a son of the World to Come" (Berachot 4b).

A lulav needs to be waved specifically to the six directions of the world, in the way that the Sages taught us. But the Torah only stated: "And you shall take for yourselves on the first day" (Leviticus 23:40). There are countless examples like these. Certainly, the Sages gave reasons for everything, but the hearts of people who want to be clever do not stand firm on this.

However, the Wisdom of Truth is what clarifies all these matters. It shows what the service is, and how far all its details reach. It shows how every small thing down here on earth goes and expands above and shakes all the worlds. Then a person will surely take it to heart, for this is the entire benefit of this wisdom.

Philosopher: I have heard in this what is sufficient for any understanding person. Now please state the first principles of this wisdom.

Initial Concepts of the Wisdom of Truth

Tzimtzum (Contraction)

Kabbalist: The beginning of everything is to know that both in the creation of the world and in its governance, the Holy One, blessed be He, did not act in the way of the Omnipotent, as He truly is, but rather in the way that people do things little by little. In this way He made and makes all existences, in this gradation.

For if He acted in the way of His omnipotence, we would not be able to speak at all about His deeds, for we would have no understanding of them at all. But since He acted in gradation, there is room for us to contemplate them.

Philosopher: This is good, and this is the tzimtzum (contraction) that we said - that the Infinite Light contracted itself so as not to enter into the matter of the creation of the world with its omnipotence, but rather in a measured way.

Kabbalist: So it is. For there are two ways for the Supreme Thought: the way of His omnipotence, and the way of gradation. Now, before He created the world, the way of gradation was not necessary. But when He wanted to create the world, that was the time for this way to be revealed. Thus, He did not want His omnipotence to enter into the creation of the world, but rather the way of gradation.

He contracted His omnipotence so as not to enter into this matter, and established the way of gradation. The parts of this way and its laws are what we understand.

Philosopher: State this matter in the terms known among the Sages of the Truth.

Kabbalist: His omnipotence we call "Infinite Light, blessed be He," meaning the Supreme Will in its completeness. The way of gradation we call "Sefirot." Thus, the Emanator, blessed be He, who is the First Existent, contracted His omnipotent will and established the way of gradation. Therefore, we say that the Infinite contracted, and then the Sefirot arose.

From here on we speak in terms of the Sefirot and their levels. For every action that is found in the lower realms, there is one root in this way of gradation, namely the Sefirot, so that when we understand all the parts of this way of gradation, we will understand the root of all that is found in the creatures and their conducts.

Lights

Philosopher: What are the Lights that the masters of this wisdom mention in this wisdom, and what is their matter?

Kabbalist: The Omnipotence, meaning what we called "the Infinite, blessed be He," we do not grasp, neither with understanding nor with vision, even prophetic vision. But the way of gradation we understand with understanding and prophetic contemplation, meaning: every law that we understand in the way of gradation, in prophetic contemplation we see one light, which means to say that law.

Thus, the entire gradation is now explained in lights, for we say there is one light whose action is such, and there is one whose action is such. It is not that the essence of the matter is light, but rather it is one law whose matter is such, and another law whose matter is such. But the laws appear in so many lights. Therefore, we speak of everything in terms of lights, but the entire matter is governance.

Philosopher: Complete the matter of the governance.

Sefirot

Kabbalist: The general laws of governance are included in ten, and all the rest are the conditions of these laws and their specifics. Since the laws appear in lights, there are ten lights found, which are the roots of the entire governance. They are called the Ten Sefirot, for when we understand them with all their parts, we will understand the entire governance.

Partsufim (Configurations)

Philosopher: And what is the matter of the Partsufim (configurations) that they mention?

Kabbalist: We can speak about the laws in general, and about the laws with all their details. The lights are either general lights that do not show their parts, or detailed lights that show their parts. However, every light that needs to act independently must reveal all its parts.

Therefore, there are ten sefirot, but according to the actions they need to perform, Partsufim are made. For example, if one light alone acts, it will reveal all its parts and be one Partsuf. If two, three, four or however many act together, between all of them the parts needed for that action will be revealed, and all of them together will be called one Partsuf.

Therefore, even if one part of the revealed parts needs to act independently and reveal its particular parts, it too will be called a Partsuf. The bottom line is that whoever has dominion and action on his own reveals his parts and is called an independent Partsuf.

For the entirety of the governance, the ten sefirot build five Partsufim: Keter acting alone becomes Arich Anpin; Chochmah - Abba; Binah - Imma; the six edges acting together become one separate Partsuf, namely Ze'ir Anpin; Malchut becomes Nukvah. There is further division, for since Malchut of Abba and Malchut of Imma dominate on their own, they too become Partsufim, namely Yisrael Saba and Tevunah. Even the malchuyot of Yisrael Saba and Tevunah become two more Partsufim. Thus, the Partsufim are: Arich Anpin, Abba and Imma, Yisrael Saba and Tevunah, Yaakov and Leah whose matters I will yet explain, and Ze'ir Anpin and his Nukvah.

Philosopher: Now explain the matters of all these according to the governance.

Masculine and Feminine - Giver and Receiver, in Their Two Stages

Kabbalist: The Supreme Will wanted to place service in the hand of man, from which would be drawn for him reward and punishment. Therefore, He placed a root for this in the governance, meaning in the way of gradation. He placed the laws of heaven and earth and all that is in them, and all that is needed for the sustenance of the entire creation. All these are revealed in the way of lights, and their entirety is called Ze'ir Anpin and his Nukvah.

These laws are not permanently fixed in one way, but rather He made it so they could be in a way of expansiveness or in a way of constriction, because of reward and punishment. If people merit, these laws will be with expansiveness: much rain, long and good life, great subjugation of enemies, great distancing of damages. If they do not merit, God forbid, all the laws will be constricted: there will only be little rain, little wealth or total poverty, and so on for all of them. Thus, according to this, these laws have many ways, ways of expansiveness and ways of constriction.

Philosopher: Speak in the terms of the Sages of Truth.

Stages of Ibur and Gadlut of the Partsuf Ze'ir Anpin

Kabbalist: The beginning of the matter is that all this is hinted to in the secret of the image of man and all his experiences. Therefore, we will speak of everything according to this way. In man there is an existence - that he is not born complete from the start, as the first man was made, but rather the fetus grows little by little. This is the secret of the gradation found in the supreme governance, the entirety of the laws of heaven and earth; they are the secret of the limbs of man in all their compositions.

Man is found at first as a small drop that goes and is completed in its limbs, but he is still closed in his mother's womb and in an incomplete state. This is the secret of the first state of these laws, which is the lowest preparation that could be. Afterwards, there is a stage where he emerges and nurses from his mother's breasts, for he still needs his mother. This shows another state for the laws. Then there is a stage where he is grown and stands on his own. This shows the complete state for the laws.

Therefore, we call the first state the ibur (gestation) of Ze'ir Anpin, the second yenikah (nursing), and the third his gadlut (maturity). This is a great principle, that every action is estimated in ten parts, which are ten sefirot. The completeness of these laws is in ten levels, which are ten sefirot. In the first state, the action is not complete, and there is only the lowest level in it, which is in the sefirot Netzach, Hod, Yesod. In nursing it is more complete, with the sefirot Chesed, Gevurah, Tiferet. In maturity: Chochmah, Binah, Da'at.

The Two Functions of Arich Anpin: Granting Existence and Complete Beneficence

There is another governance which is the governance of sustenance, meaning that it is impossible for the world to always stand entirely according to the deeds of the lower beings, for it would be destroyed many times. Therefore, there is one governance that is entirely according to the attribute of kindness and its matters, to do kindness in general, and to provide for every place where the attribute of judgment would not allow the world to be improved - this complete kindness would benefit.

This governance is called Arich Anpin, and it always stands in one balance in which there are no changes of times. All that is there is either that it will be revealed or that it will not be revealed, meaning: the kindness acts in concealment, for "a king establishes the land with justice" (Proverbs 29:4), but he conceals his thought, which is the kindness, and with this the world endures. Sometimes he reveals the attribute of his goodness and benefits openly without any concealment. There are also known, fixed ways for this, both in what suffices for the governance so the world will not be destroyed, and in what is needed at times to act with revealed kindness.

Judgment Stems from and is Sweetened by Arich Anpin

However, you must know that the beginning of His will, blessed be He, is to benefit. But in order to benefit with a complete benefit, with justice, so that in the end it will truly be a benefit, like a father who afflicts his son in order to benefit him in his end, the judgment itself emerges and is born from the kindness that we mentioned. However, there are also ways for this, meaning from which aspects that exist in the beneficence does this matter of judgment emerge. This chain itself is a matter to understand on its own, and this is called Abba and Imma.

The Stages of Judgment: Arich Anpin, Abba and Imma, Ze'ir Anpin and Nukvah

The entirety of the governance is found to be three levels: First, the attribute of complete kindness in all its aspects, wanting to benefit all, namely Arich Anpin. However, there is one aspect there that causes the need for judgment, and that is because the benefit must be complete, and it is not complete if the receivers do not receive it with complete reward. For if not, they are embarrassed in receiving it. Thus, matters must be considered according to the benefit itself - how the judgment will be built in its parts.

The judgment itself in all its aspects is Ze'ir Anpin and Nukvah, meaning the Nukvah according to the aspect of the receivers, in proportion to their preparation, and Ze'ir Anpin is the aspect of the bestowal. What is in between, meaning the way this judgment emerges from the beneficence, is Abba and Imma. Thus, Abba and Imma are nothing but the causes of this judgment according to the first law of beneficence.

Now the profound counsel is revealed before us: The Supreme Will wanted to bestow to all a complete beneficence, and this attribute is Arich Anpin. However, from here emerges the matter of judgment that must exist, and there are some known ways to make this judgment, and the judgment is built according to them. Thus, the judgment and its ways of coming into being are found, so that we may discern each thing on its own.

When we want to understand the roots of this judgment, meaning the roots of these laws, how they are founded, we must discern Abba and Imma and all their aspects. But when we want to know the laws themselves, what they are, we understand Ze'ir Anpin. You will see that beneficences give birth to their consequences, and therefore Abba and Imma are what produce Ze'ir Anpin and Nukvah.

Abba is the distant cause, the first cause. Imma is the proximate cause, the second cause. The beginning of judgment is the complete law, but since the matter goes according to the aspect of beneficence, these laws must be completed, meaning they must approach the beneficence. Therefore, matters proceed and are completed, namely the attribute of judgment and its appeasement.

Therefore, ibur (gestation) is the beginning of the existence of judgment, and it is the complete law. Yenikah (nursing) is the more sweetened law, for the appeasement has begun. The end of the appeasement is gadlut (maturity), and it is the revelation of how the law itself is made only to benefit. This entire governance is always explained in the secret of the image of man. Thus, let us mention everything in human terms, both in limbs and in movements, and in all conducts, including all of this...

Philosopher: Indeed, this way is very straight to begin with, and from here a person can go afterwards to study the chapters, and afterwards to the Openings of Wisdom with their explanations.

However, now complete the explanation of what is before Atzilut and what is after it. You still need to explain the unions within Atzilut itself.

Kabbalist: Why did you first ask about what is before Atzilut and after it, and afterwards about the unions which are in Atzilut itself?

Philosopher: Because the unions are a general matter in all the worlds. Therefore, I will first ask you to explain the worlds themselves, and afterwards the unions that are in all of them.

Adam Kadmon, Atik, the World of Atzilut

Kabbalist: I will answer you each thing in order, and first what is before Atzilut. I spoke of the conducts that are needed for this world, but the end of things is not here, but rather after six thousand years, meaning the World of Reward. For the Garden of Eden is not the World of Reward, for only the soul is there, but after the resurrection of the dead there will be the reward, where the soul and also the body will be. This too is an attribute in itself. This world compared to the World to Come is like a corridor before a hall. What they serve in this world must be fixed for the need of the reward in the World to Come.

Here there are two things: the attribute of reward in the secret of the World to Come, and the passageway between this world and the World to Come, where the deeds of here will be fixed there. The World to Come is a matter above Atzilut, outside of the service. For this matter, there is the world of the Infinite, called Adam Kadmon, and all that depends on it, and Atzilut is a corridor before it. The Malchut of Adam Kadmon comes to Atzilut and clothes in it. This is the connection and the passageway that I mentioned, which is between the world of service and the world of reward, and this is called Atik.

Thus, the entire existence is now found: Adam Kadmon and all that depends on it, Atik which is its Malchut, the five Partsufim in Atzilut and all their divisions, which are the entirety of the entire governance. The beginning of thought is the end of deed, for the ultimate purpose is the reward in the future to come, for the entire desire of the unique Master is only to benefit.

This attribute of His goodness is the first matter, namely Adam Kadmon and all that depends on it, as mentioned above. However, in order to come to the hall, the corridor was needed because of the service that would be found, and this is the world of Atzilut that emerges from Adam Kadmon. The Malchut of Adam Kadmon is the connection between this and that, as mentioned above.

Atzilut itself - the first governance in it is kindness, for the Holy One, blessed be He, did not place judgment in the world if kindness did not precede it at first. On the contrary, the entire intent is to benefit, and this is Arich Anpin. However, from there emerges further the matter of judgment, namely the roots of judgment and its causes, and these are Abba and Imma.

Afterwards, the judgment is in its own laws, and these are Ze'ir Anpin and Nukvah. The changes in all these lights are the changes in the ways of all these laws.

Philosopher: You explained well what precedes Atzilut. Now explain what was before Atzilut at the time of the deed.

The World of Nekudim, the Shattering, the World of Tikkun

Kabbalist: Until we come to the matter of service, there is no good and evil there. But when we come to this, the matter of good and evil must be renewed, and this is simple. However, this is a great principle: As long as the cause bestows to its effect, the power of the cause will be strong, and when the cause is concealed, the consequence will not stand.

The Supreme Will wanted to place existence and extinction in the world. So He prepared all this in this way, meaning: First, the very cause for the existences. Afterwards, He gave room for the concealment of these causes, so the effects would remain nullified. Afterwards, He again revealed these causes with the proper power.

In the concealment of the causes, the very concealment of the cause of existence became the cause of extinction, and this is simple. According to the types of concealments that were made, so many types of causes were made for extinction. Thus, in preparing the Supreme Will with the causes of existence, the lights that illuminated were illuminating. With their concealment, the lights were as if nullified and darkened, and this itself became the cause of extinction. The concealment of existence is the cause of extinction.

Afterwards, the causes of existence were again revealed, and the causes of extinction were also removed as before. This is the preparation for what is needed in this world. This means that the end of the correction of the world will be with only the causes of existence remaining, without any existence of concealment of causes at all. Then there will no longer be evil in the world.

Philosopher: Speak according to the words of the Wisdom of Truth.

Kabbalist: We say that ten sefirot emerged at first, and they are what we call the World of Nekudim (Points), which were the causes of all the existences in this world. They were shattered and nullified, and this is the concealment of the cause that we mentioned. From that shattering, all the corruptions were born.

Afterwards, the sefirot were repaired, and this world was made as it is now, meaning the tikkun (repair) is that which gave room for existence. However, since a complete tikkun was not made, therefore corruptions still remained in the world. When the tikkun will be complete, there will no longer be any evil at all in the world. When we want to know the matters of good and evil and the general repairs of the world, we will go and seek them in the matter of the shattering and the tikkun.

Philosopher: And from where did these sefirot emerge?

The Sefirot Emerged from Adam Kadmon

Kabbalist: The entirety of all the governance whose beginning is in thought is the World of Reward. Afterwards are all the other times that precede it in deed. The entirety of all this is what we call Adam Kadmon. From this Adam Kadmon emerge these sefirot, from which afterwards the world of Atzilut is made, the world of service, as mentioned above.

This means to say that even this world, its cause is the World of Reward, which is the ultimate purpose. For in order to reach it, this matter of service is needed. Therefore, we say that Atzilut emerges from Adam Kadmon, from that aspect of reward in it that causes this, meaning from what is needed for the beneficence to be without embarrassment, etc. From that matter, this matter was chained, and they are these sefirot. All the matter that we mentioned was in them.

Philosopher: Speak of the way of tikkun.

The Way of Tikkun

Kabbalist: Since the causes were nullified and concealed, there was no existence for the existences to be found. On the contrary, the causes of extinction were revealed. Afterwards, the causes of existence were again being revealed, and all the levels and laws were being revealed one by one, meaning first the levels of Arich Anpin, and afterwards Abba and Imma, and so on.

All this was also with the aid of another light that was revealed, called the new MA"H, whose matter is what causes strength to the causes to be revealed and not be nullified. This gave repair to the causes that we mentioned, so they would not be concealed but would be revealed and act their actions.

The causes that we mentioned were being clarified, for each one to be in its function over its proper action. However, the extinction was not nullified from the world. Rather, at the end of all the levels, some causes bringing forth the corruptions in the world remained, and from them emerged the Sitra Achra, which is what makes all the evils in the world, as will be explained below...

Philosopher: You explained what precedes Atzilut. Now explain what is after it.

The Worlds of Atzilut and the Worlds of Beriah, Yetzirah and Asiyah

Kabbalist: Atzilut is the measures of the Supreme Thought, which are the roots of the creatures and their governance. For the types of creatures are themselves like the types of laws that are in the governance. Each creature indicates one part of the laws of the governance. Thus, that law is the root of that creature. Therefore, Atzilut is called the root of all existences.

However, the actual existences are from Beriah and below. In Beriah, there is the Divinity, blessed be He, namely the ten sefirot themselves that shine their radiance. From that radiance, the servants standing to bring out the decree of the Supreme Thought into actuality receive. For so did the Supreme Will desire, that the acts would be actualized through servants, the emissaries of the King, upon whom the Supreme King rides. The radiance of the sefirot that we mentioned rides upon the angel and brings the matter out into actuality. For each individual mission, one angel is found to do it.

Beriah, Yetzirah, Asiyah are three worlds, one below the other, where the creations sit in gradation, the upper ones above and the lower ones below them, and those yet lower, further below. In all of them there is the radiance of the sefirot themselves, revealed there in each place according to what it is, meaning: Above, the radiance shines, and from there receive the servants who are lesser than the upper ones, until man and all the physicality in the lowest of all worlds are found.

Penimiut (Innerness), Chitzoniyut (Externality) and Or Makif (Surrounding Light)

Philosopher: You still need to explain the matter of penimiut (innerness) and chitzoniyut (externality), and or makif (surrounding light).

Kabbalist: All the sefirot are the actions acted upon by the Creator, blessed be He, to His creations. In them there is what relates to the actor and what relates to the acted upon. This is penimiut and chitzoniyut, and it is itself light and vessel. Since the actor oversees every side, therefore the light is found inside, meaning concealed within, and surrounding from outside, meaning overseeing from outside. These are or penimi (inner light) and or makif.

To understand this matter in detail is the secret of the root of body and soul in man. The vessels are the root of the body, and therefore all the matters dependent on the body are rooted in them. The light within them, or surrounding them, is the root of the soul. However, when we go to gradation, we find that the penimiut is much higher in value than the chitzoniyut, like the value of the soul compared to the body.

But when we evaluate a lower level compared to the one above it, we say that the end of the chitzoniyut in the upper level is the penimiut in the lower level. In all of them, the lower one is lower than the upper one. Therefore, we say that Netzach, Hod, Yesod of Imma are the mochin (mental faculties) for Ze'ir Anpin, and likewise those of Ze'ir Anpin for the Nukvah.

Unions

Philosopher: Now explain the unions.

Kabbalist: The root of the entire governance is right and left, meaning kindness and judgment. The governance needs to emerge with the agreement of both. The extension of all the laws, in the proper order, in the aspect of kindness, is the male. Their extension, also in order, in the aspect of judgment, is the female. These need to join together.

The beginning of the progeny emerging is from the first power in the mind, and it extends and chains from all the powers - one drop, in which all are included, which is man - his 613 limbs. It emerges to the right and to the left.

The law is what dominates more to influence the world, for the world was created with law, but He partnered with it also the governance of kindness and its dominion. This is the female receiving from the male. It is bestowed upon the world, which is conducted with law as mentioned above, through the female, as we said.

Since there are many levels of kindness and judgment, therefore the lights, and according to their weakness, in the secret of gradation, many types of unions were fixed, all in gradation, each greater than the other, to bestow upon the worlds many types of bestowal, one more than the other, as needed in all the times.

Philosopher: This is certainly enough to give the first depiction of the wisdom, and the rest of the explanation - one who desires to descend to the depth of things, let him go in the straight path that you have prepared in your chapters and your openings. "And God gives wisdom from His mouth, knowledge and understanding" (based on Proverbs 2:6). Amen, so may it be His will.

The Books of the Ramchal

The Ramchal wrote more than eighty books on Kabbalah, ethics, morality, philosophy, and more. Most of his books have been lost and today we are only aware of these books

סוד ה' ליראיו	מסילת ישרים
תקט"ו תפילות	דרך ה'
תיקונים חדשים	מאמר העיקרים
קיצור כוונות	דרך חכמה.
עיקרי הדינים	דרך עץ החיים
אגרות רמח"ל	דרך תבונות
ירים משה	דעת תבונות
ספר השירים	ספר הכללים
שרשי המצוות	קל"ח פתחי חכמה
ספרי דקדוק ומליצה	קנאת ה' צבאות
לשון לימודים	אדיר במרום
ספר ההגיון	משכני עליון
ספר המליצה	מאמר הגאולה
ספר הדקדוק	זוהר תנינא
מחזות קודש:	עשרה אורות
מעשה שמשון	פנות המרכבה
מגדל עז או תומת ישרים.	האילן הקדוש
לישרים תהילה	מאמר הוויכוח
בנין עולם	חוקר ומקובל
פתחי חכמה ודעת	מלחמת משה
	רזין גניזין

Description of Some Books of the Ramchal

Adir Bamarom

Adir Bamarom by the Ramchal is a commentary on the section Adrah Rabah of the Zohar. which is a seminal text in the study of Kabbalah. The Ramchal aims to clarify and elaborate on the Zohar's teachings. Each section builds upon the previous one, leading the reader to a more profound understanding of kabbalistic thought and concepts.

Derech Eitz Chaim

Derech Eitz Chaim (The Way of the Tree of Life) is a profound guide to Jewish meditation and prayer. It is not divided into chapters in a modern sense but is rather a continuous discourse divided into sections that deal with various aspects of spiritual practice and prayer. The text is aimed at guiding the reader towards achieving a closer communion with the Divine through a deeper understanding and practice of the mitzvot (commandments) and prayer, with a particular focus on the kavanot (mystical intentions).

Hokhmat HaEmet

"Hokhmat HaEmet" (The Wisdom of Truth) is a work about the exploration of Kabbalistic truth and delves into the Ramchal's understanding of divine wisdom as it pertains to the nature of God, creation, and the path to spiritual enlightenment. It also contains a series of discourses on various topics within Jewish mysticism and philosophy.

Messilat Yesharim

Messilat Yesharim - Way of the Justs by Rabbi Moshe Chaim Luzzatto - the Ramchal, is a classic work of Jewish ethical literature. Written in the 18th century. It is a practical guide to moral and spiritual growth, rooted in the Mussar tradition. It's structured around the steps one must climb to reach spiritual perfection.

Each chapter in "Messilat Yesharim" is designed to be a stepping stone, gradually leading the reader from fundamental concepts to more advanced stages of spiritual growth and moral excellence. This work is characterized by its clarity, practicality, and depth, offering guidance that is as relevant today as it was when it was written.

Klach Pitchei Chochmah

Klach Pitchei Chochmah - 138 Openings of Wisdom is a Kabbalistic text that is complex and dense, containing deep mystical insights into the nature of the divine and the universe. The text is not structured in a typical chapter format, but rather as individual entries or "openings" that explore various aspects of Kabbalistic wisdom. These openings are concise sections, each discussing different elements of the Sefirotic system, the structure of the divine realms, and the interplay between the physical and the spiritual.

Ma'amar HaGeulah

Ma'amar HaGeulah, or "Discourse on the Redemption," is a kabbalistic exposition on the themes of exile and redemption as they pertain to both individual spiritual states and the collective destiny of the Jewish people and the world, particularly those concerning the ultimate redemption or 'Geulah.'

Migdal Oz

Migdal Oz, which translates to "Strong Tower," is another one of the Ramchal's kabbalistic works. The title itself suggests a focus on strength and fortitude in the spiritual realm, likely drawing from Proverbs 18:10, "The name of the Lord is a strong tower; the righteous run into it and are safe." It contains a series of interconnected discussions or essays on various spiritual and mystical themes and also includes intricate discussions of divine emanations and the ways in which they interact with the world and humanity.

Kinat Hashem Tzevaot

Kinat Hashem Tzevaot - "The Zeal of the Lord of Hosts." This work discusses the passionate commitment of God to His purposes and plans, particularly as it relates to the defense of His honor and the fulfillment of His will through the history of Israel and the unfolding of the cosmos. And the divine zeal as it pertains to the rectification and purification of the world, leading to the final redemption.

Sod Hageulah

Sod Hageulah - Secrets of Redemption is in line with Ramchal's kabbalistic philosophy, it likely explores the deeper spiritual dimensions of redemption (Geulah), both personal and collective. It blends profound kabbalistic insights with practical guidance, encouraging readers to live with an awareness of the redemptive process and to participate in it through spiritual growth and ethical conduct. Each section would build upon the last, forming a comprehensive picture of the Ramchal's vision of

Sefer HaKavanot

Sefer HaKavanot, which translates to "The Book of Intentions," is a mystical manual that delves into the kavanot, or specific mystical intentions and meditations, one should have during the performance of Jewish prayers and commandments (mitzvot). The Ramchal, in this text, elaborates on the profound spiritual roots of Jewish practices and how each act can be a conduit for drawing down divine influences and rectifying the various spiritual realms.

Zohar Tinyana

Zohar Tinyana, -The Second Zohar, is an extension of the themes found in the classic Zohar, written in a similar style. The Ramchal uses the form of a mystical commentary to delve deeper into the secrets of the Torah, expanding upon the spiritual and ethical teachings contained within the original Zohar.

Ma'amar HaVikuach

Ma'amar HaVikuach - The Kabbalist and the Philosopher is a philosophical work by the Ramchal. This work is structured as a dialogue between a philosopher and a Kabbalist and is intended to defend the Kabbalistic worldview against philosophical criticisms.

The Ramchal uses this dialogue to reconcile the seemingly divergent paths of rational philosophy and mystical tradition, arguing that Kabbalah provides a deeper understanding of the world that complements rather than contradicts rational thought.

The philosopher in the dialogue represents the rationalist approach, seeking to understand the world through logic and observation. In contrast, the Kabbalist represents the mystical tradition, which includes esoteric knowledge and divine revelation as sources of truth.

Da'at Tevunot

Da'at Tevunot -The Wisdom of Consciouness is one of the major works of the Ramchal. The book is structured as a dialogue between the intellect and the soul, exploring the nature of divine wisdom and justice. It addresses profound questions about God's management of the world, the purpose of creation, the role of mankind, and the process of redemption.

Samples of books of the Ramchal translated by Rav Raphael Afilalo

The Way of the Justs - Mesilat Yesharim
God and his Ways - Derekh Hashem
The Wisdom of Consciousness - Daat Tevunot

The Way of the Justs – Mesilat Yesharim

The Way of the Justs, is a classic work of Jewish ethical literature. Written in the 18th century. It is a practical guide to moral and spiritual growth, rooted in the Mussar tradition. It's structured around the steps one must climb to reach spiritual perfection.

Each chapter is designed to be a stepping stone, gradually leading the reader from fundamental concepts to more advanced stages of spiritual growth and moral excellence. This work is characterized by its clarity, practicality, and depth, offering guidance that is as relevant today as it was when it was written.

The author said: I did not compose this work to teach people what they do not know, but to remind them of what is already known and widely publicized among them. For you will not find in most of my words anything but matters that most people know and do not doubt at all. However, just as these matters are widely known and their truth is clear to all, forgetfulness of them is also very common and prevalent. Therefore, the benefit derived from this book does not come from reading it once, for it is possible that the reader will not find novel ideas in his mind after reading it that were not there before reading it, except a little. Rather, the benefit comes from reviewing it and persevering with it, for these matters that are naturally forgotten by people will be remembered, and one will take to heart one's duty which one overlooks.

If you consider the current state of most of the world, you will see that most people of quick understanding and sharp intellect apply most of their analysis and contemplation to the intricacies of different wisdoms and the depth of theoretical studies, each person according to his intellectual inclination and natural desire. Some exert great effort in studying the creation and nature, while others devote all of their theoretical analysis to astronomy and geometry, and others to crafts. Yet others delve further into the holy, that is, the study of the sacred Torah -- some in the give and take of halachic discussions, some in midrashim, and some in halachic rulings. But few belong to the category that establishes the study and analysis of matters of perfection in divine service, of love, fear, attachment, and all the other aspects of piety (chassidut).

This is not because these matters are not fundamental principles to them, for if you ask them, each one will say that this is the main principle. One cannot imagine a truly wise person for whom all these matters are not clear. Rather, the reason that they do not apply much analysis to it is due to the matters being so well-known and simple to them that they do not see a need to spend much time analyzing them. The study of these matters and the reading of books of this type is left only to those whose intellect is not so sharp and close to being coarse. You will see them diligent in all this and not budging from it, to the point that according to the practice prevalent in the world, when you see a pious individual, you cannot avoid suspecting him of being of coarse intellect.

However, the results of this practice are very detrimental for both the wise and the unwise, for it causes both to lack true piety, making it very rare to find in the world. It is lacking in the wise due to their limited analysis of it, and lacking in the unwise due to their limited grasp of it. As a result, most people imagine that piety depends on reciting many psalms, very long confessions, difficult fasts, and immersions in ice and snow -- all matters with which the intellect is not content and the mind is not at ease.

True piety, which is desirable and pleasant, is far from our conceptual image. It is a simple matter -- that which is not a person's obligation, he does not have in mind. Even though its basic principles are already fixed in the heart of every upright person, if he does not engage in them, he will see their details without recognizing them; he will encounter them without noticing them. See that matters of piety and matters of fear and love and purity of heart are not matters ingrained in a person such that he does not need means to acquire them. People do not find them on their own just as they find all of their natural functions like sleep and wakefulness, hunger and satiety, and all the other functions engraved in our nature. Rather, they certainly require means and strategies to acquire them, and there are also factors that detract from them and distance them from a person. There is no lack of ways to distance their detriments. If so, how can one not need to spend time analyzing this matter in order to know the truth of these matters, to know the way to acquire them and uphold them? From where will this wisdom come into a person's heart if he does not seek it?

Once the need for perfection in divine service and the obligation of its purity and cleanliness has been affirmed by every wise person -- for without these it is certainly not desired at all, but despised and abhorred, as "the L-rd searches all hearts and understands the inclination of all thoughts" (Chronicles 1:29:17) -- how will we respond on the day of rebuke if we were negligent in this analysis and abandoned a matter that is so incumbent upon us, as it is the essence of what the L-rd our G-d asks of us? Is it conceivable that our intellect would toil and labor in analyses that we are not obligated in, in give-and-takes from which we derive no benefit, and in laws that do not apply to us, while we leave the great duty that we owe to our Creator to habit and treat it as rote learned from others? If we did not contemplate and analyze what is true fear and its branches, how will we acquire it and how will we escape from the worldly vanity that causes us to forget it?

Will it not be forgotten and lost even though we know it is our duty? Love, likewise -- if we do not strive to instill it in our hearts with the force of all the means that bring us to it, how will we find it within us? From where will attachment and passion for Him, may He be blessed, and His Torah come into our souls if we do not pay heed to His greatness and His exaltedness, which give birth to this attachment in our hearts? How will our thoughts be purified if we do not strive to cleanse them of the blemishes that the physical nature inflicts upon them, along with all of the character traits that likewise require correction and straightening -- who will straighten them and who will correct them if we do not pay attention to them and do not examine the matter with great precision? Indeed, if we would analyze the matter with true analysis, we would find it in its true form and benefit ourselves, and we would teach it to others and benefit them as well.

This is as Solomon said: "If you seek it like silver and search for it as for treasures, then you will understand the fear of the L-rd" (Proverbs 2:4-5). He does not say, "Then you will understand philosophy, then you will understand astronomy, then you will understand medicine, then you will understand laws, then you will understand halachot," but rather, "Then you will understand the fear of the L-rd." You see that in order to understand fear, you must seek it like silver and search for it like treasures. Indeed, in what we have been taught by our forefathers and in what is well-known to every intelligent person in general terms -- will time be found for all other areas of analysis but not for this analysis? Why should a person not set aside times, at the very least, for this contemplation, if he is compelled to turn to other analyses or pursuits in the rest of his time?

The verse states, "Behold, the fear of the Lord is wisdom" (Job 28:28), and our Sages, may their memory be for a blessing, said (Shabbat 31b): "'Behold' means one, as in Greek they call 'one' hen." We see that fear is wisdom, and it alone is wisdom. Certainly, that which does not involve analysis is not called wisdom. But the truth is that great analysis is needed for all these matters -- to know them truthfully and not by imagination and false reasoning, and all the more so to acquire them and attain them.

One who contemplates them will see that piety does not depend on those matters that the foolish pietists imagine, but on matters of true perfection and great wisdom. This is what Moses our teacher, peace be upon him, teaches us when he says: "And now, Israel, what does the Lord your G-d ask of you, but to fear the Lord your G-d, to walk in all His ways, and to love Him, and to serve the Lord your G-d with all your heart and with all your soul, to keep the commandments of the Lord and His statutes?" (Deuteronomy 10:12). Here he encapsulated all the elements of the perfection of the service that is desirable to His blessed Name, which are: fear, walking in His ways, love, wholeness of heart, and observing all the commandments.

Fear is the awe of His exaltedness, may He be blessed, such that one fears Him as one would fear a great and awesome king, and is embarrassed before His greatness with regard to every movement that one is about to make, and certainly when speaking before Him in prayer or engaging in His Torah. Walking in His ways includes the entire matter of the rectitude of one's character traits and their correction, and this is what they, may their memory be for a blessing, explained: "Just as He is merciful, so should you be merciful" (Shabbat 133b), and the general principle of all this is that a person should conduct all of his character traits and all types of his actions according to integrity and morality. Our Sages, may their memory be for a blessing, encapsulated it as "All that brings glory to its Maker and glory to him from man" (Avot 2:1), meaning all that leads to the ultimate true good, meaning that its outcome is the reinforcement of the Torah and the betterment of the fellowship of states. Love is that love for Him, may He be blessed, should be instilled in a person's heart to the point that his soul is aroused to do what is pleasing before Him, just as one's heart is aroused to do what is pleasing to his father and mother, and he is distressed if this is lacking on his part or on the part of others, and he is zealous for this and rejoices greatly when he does something of this.

Wholeness of heart means that the service before Him, may He be blessed, should be with purity of intent, meaning for the sole purpose of serving Him and not for any other motive. Included in this is that one should be whole in service and not like one who hobbles between two opinions or like one who performs the commandments by rote, but that one's entire heart should be devoted to this. Observing all the commandments: As its literal meaning, that is, observing all the commandments with all their details and conditions.

Now, all these are general principles that require great explanation. I found that our Sages, may their memory be for a blessing, summarized these parts in a different order, more detailed and arranged according to the necessary progression in acquiring them properly. This is what they said in a baraita, cited in various places in the Talmud, one of them in the chapter "Before Their Festivals." These are their words: "From here Rabbi Pinchas ben Yair said: Torah leads to watchfulness, watchfulness leads to alacrity, alacrity leads to cleanliness, cleanliness leads to separation, separation leads to purity, purity leads to piety, piety leads to humility, humility leads to fear of sin, fear of sin leads to holiness, holiness leads to Divine inspiration, Divine inspiration leads to the resurrection of the dead."

Based on this baraita, I decided to compose this work to teach myself and remind others of the conditions for perfect service, according to their levels. I will explain regarding each one its matters and parts or details, the way to acquire it and what detracts from it, and the way to be vigilant against them. For I will read it, and so will all who find contentment in it, so that we may learn to fear the L-rd our G-d, and our duty before Him will not be forgotten by us. And that which the corporeality of nature strives to remove from our heart, the reading and contemplation will bring to our memory and arouse us to what we are commanded. May the L-rd be our support and guard our feet from being trapped, and may the request of the psalmist, beloved to his G-d, be fulfilled in us: "Teach me Your way, O Lord, that I may walk in Your truth; unite my heart to fear Your Name" (Psalms 86:11). Amen, may this be His will.

Chapter 1 - Explaining the general obligation of a person in his world

The foundation of piety and the root of complete service is for a person to clarify and verify what his duty is in his world and toward what he should place his outlook and aspiration in all that he toils for all the days of his life. What our Sages of blessed memory have taught us is that man was only created to delight in G-d and to bask in the radiance of His Presence, for this is the true delight and the greatest of all pleasures that can be found. The place of this delight is truly in the World to Come, for it was created with the preparation needed for this.

However, the means to arrive at this desired destination is this world. This is what they, of blessed memory, said (Avot 4:16): "This world is like a vestibule before the World to Come." The means that bring a person to this ultimate purpose are the mitzvot which G-d, blessed be His Name, has commanded us to perform. The place of performing the mitzvot is only in this world. Therefore, man was placed in this world first, so that through these means that are available to him here, he can reach the place that was prepared for him, which is the World to Come, to delight there in the goodness that he acquired through these means. This is what they said, of blessed memory

(Eruvin 22a): "Today is for doing them and tomorrow is for receiving reward."

When you contemplate the matter, you will see that true perfection is only attachment to Him, blessed be He, and this is what King David would say (Psalms 73:28): "But as for me, G-d's nearness is my good." And he says (ibid. 27:4): "One thing I ask of the L-rd, that I seek - that I may dwell in the House of the L-rd all the days of my life, etc." For only this is good, and all that people consider good besides this is vain and deceptive foolishness. However, when a person merits this goodness, it is fitting that he first toil and strive with exertion to acquire it. That is, he should strive to attach himself to Him, blessed be He, through the power of deeds that lead to this matter, and these are the mitzvot.

Now, the Holy One, Blessed be He, has placed man in a location where many things distance him from Him, blessed be He, and these are the material desires; if he is drawn after them, behold, he distances himself and moves away from the true good. Thus, he is truly placed amidst the fierce battle, for all matters of the world, whether for good or bad, are tests for man. Poverty on one hand and wealth on the other hand, as Solomon said (Proverbs 30:9): "Lest I become sated and deny and say, 'Who is the L-rd?', and lest I become impoverished and steal, etc." Tranquility on one hand and suffering on the other hand, until the battle is found before him and behind him. If he will be a man of valor and triumph in the war from all sides, he will be the perfect man who will merit to attach himself to his Creator and emerge from this vestibule to enter the palace to bask in the light of life. To the degree that he conquered his evil inclination and desires and distanced himself from what distances him from the good and strove to attach himself to Him, so will he attain Him and rejoice in Him.

If you delve further into the matter, you will see that the world was created for the use of man. However, it stands in great balance. For if man is drawn after the world and distances himself from his Creator, behold, he deteriorates and causes the world to deteriorate with him. But if he rules over himself and attaches himself to his Creator and uses the world only to assist him in the service of his Creator, he elevates himself and the world itself is elevated with him. For it is indeed a great elevation for all creatures to be of service to the perfect man who is sanctified with His sanctity, blessed be He. This is like the matter that our Sages, may their memory be for a blessing, said regarding the light that the Holy One, Blessed be He, stored away for the righteous, and these are their words (Chagiga 12a): "When the Holy One, Blessed be He, saw the light that He stored away for the righteous, He rejoiced, as it is stated (Proverbs 13:9): 'The light of the righteous will rejoice.'"

Regarding the stones that Yaakov took and placed around his head, they said (Chullin 91b): "Rebbi Yitzchak said: This teaches that they all gathered together into one place and each one said, 'Upon me the righteous one will rest his head.'"

Our Sages of blessed memory have indeed alerted us to this fundamental in the Midrash Kohelet (Rabba 7:13), where they said, these are their words: "'See the work of G-d, etc.' (Kohelet 7:13). "When the Holy One, Blessed be He, created Adam the first man, He took him and led him round all the trees of the Garden of Eden and said to him: Behold My works, how beautiful and praiseworthy they are! All that I have created, I created for your sake. Pay attention that you do not corrupt and destroy My world."

In summary, man was not created for his situation in this world, but for his situation in the World to Come. However, his situation in this world is a means for his situation in the World to Come, which is the ultimate purpose. Therefore, you will find that the statements of our Sages, may their memory be for a blessing, are numerous and they all follow one style, likening this world to a place and time of preparation, and the World to Come to the place of rest and eating what is already prepared. This is what they said: "This world is similar to a vestibule" (Avot 4:16), as they said, of blessed memory: "Today is for doing them and tomorrow is for receiving reward" (Eruvin 22a). "One who toiled on Shabbat eve will eat on Shabbat" (Avodah Zara 3a). "This world is similar to dry land and the World to Come to the sea, etc." (Kohelet Rabba 1:15). There are many such statements along this line.

You can truly see that no intelligent person could believe that the purpose of man's creation is for his situation in this world. For what is man's life in this world, and who is truly happy and tranquil in this world? "The days of our years among them are seventy years, and if with might, eighty years; but their pride is toil and pain" (Psalms 90:10) - with many types of pain, illnesses, ailments and troubles, and after all this, death. Not one out of a thousand is found for whom the world grants many pleasures and true tranquility, and even he, if he lives to a hundred years, has already passed and is negated from the world.

Moreover, if the purpose of man's creation were for his situation in this world, there would be no need for instilling in him such an important and lofty soul that would be greater even than the angels themselves, all the more so since it finds no satisfaction in any worldly pleasures. This is what they taught us, of blessed memory, in Midrash Kohelet, these are their words (Kohelet Rabba 6:6): "'And also the soul will not be filled' - To what is the matter comparable? To a villager who married a princess. If he brings her everything in the world, it is worth nothing to her, for she is a princess. So too the soul - if you bring it all the delicacies of the world, they are nothing to it. Why? Because it comes from above."

Similarly, our Rabbis, may their memory be for a blessing, said (Avot 4:22): "Against your will you were created and against your will you were born." For the soul does not at all love this world; on the contrary, it despises it. If so, the Creator, blessed be He, certainly would not create a creation for a purpose that is against its nature and despised by it. Rather, man's creation is for his condition in the World to Come. Therefore, this soul was placed in him, for it is fitting for it to serve, and through it man can receive reward in its place and time, so that nothing despised will befall his soul in this world. On the contrary, it will be loved and cherished by it. This is simple.

Now that we know this, we immediately understand the severity of the mitzvot that are upon us and the preciousness of the service that is in our hands. For behold, these are the means that bring us to true perfection, without which it cannot be attained at all. However, it is known that the goal is not reached except through the power of assembling all the means that were found and that served to reach it. According to the power of the means and their utilization, so will be the goal born of them. Any slight difference found in the means, its outcome will certainly be discerned with clarity when the time of the goal born of the assembly of all of them arrives, as I wrote, and this is clear. From now on, it is certain that the precision with which one must be exacting regarding the mitzvot and service must be with the utmost precision, as weighers of gold and pearls are exacting due to their great value. For their outcome is born in true perfection and eternal preciousness, above which there is no greater preciousness.

We have thus learned that the main existence of man in this world is only to fulfill mitzvot, serve, and withstand trials. The pleasures of the world should not be for him except merely as an aid and assistance, so that he will have contentment and peace of mind in order to turn his heart to this service that is incumbent upon him. Indeed, it is fitting for him that his entire orientation should be only to the blessed Creator, and he should have no other purpose in any act he performs, small or large, except to draw close to Him, blessed be He, and to break down all the barriers that separate him from his Maker. These are all matters of materiality and what depends on them, until he is drawn after Him, blessed be He, literally like iron after a magnet. Whatever he can think of as a means for this closeness, he should pursue it and grasp it and not let go of it.

And whatever he can think of as a hindrance to this, he should flee from it as one flees from fire. As it is said (Psalms 63:9): "My soul cleaves after You; Your right hand upholds me." Since his coming to the world is only for this purpose, namely, to attain this closeness by rescuing his soul from all that prevents it and causes it to lose out, now that we know and have clarified for ourselves the truth of this principle, we must examine its details according to their levels, from the beginning of the matter to its end, as Rabbi Pinchas ben Yair arranged them in his statement that we already cited in our introduction. They are: watchfulness, alacrity, cleanliness, separation, purity, piety, humility, fear of sin, and holiness. Now we will explain them one by one with the help of Heaven.

God and his Ways - Derekh Hashem

Introduction by the Ramchal

The sublime advantage of comprehending reality through grasping the precise configuration and interrelation of its constituent parts, rather than viewing it as an undifferentiated whole, is akin to the difference between observing an orderly garden beautifully arranged into beds, paths and rows, versus seeing a chaotic thicket or tangled forest. For though one may conceptualize many parts whose authentic connections and positioning within the integrated structure remains unknown, this leaves the intellect that yearns for true understanding burdened without satisfaction. Each element pictured in isolation excites curiosity about its completion within the whole, yet its deficient portrayal precludes this, thus troubling the mind and paining it with unquenched longing and unremitting confusion.

In dramatic contrast, one who properly discerns the nature of each part according to its various aspects beholds the subject unveiled before him in its fullness. The intellect then delights, following wherever interest leads within the beauty of its composition, as coherent comprehension is attained. For integral to properly understanding any topic is recognizing its essence and distinguishing parameters.

Thus, one must firstly determine the fundamental categorization and station of each element within the framework of reality. The primordial classifications are: whole or part; generality or particular; cause or effect; conveyer or addon. Correspondingly, initial analysis of any subject must establish whether it is a complete entity or constituent component; a universal principle or specific detail; an originating cause or resultant outcome; an underlying substrate or accrued attribute.

Profoundly, the precise aspects warranting examination stem from its innate properties and role. If part, one must identify the whole it helps comprise. If particular, its belonging generality is sought. Effects are traced to causes, and causes to antecedents. Adjuncts are scrutinized in light of their bearer. Additionally, the adjunct's nature is examined - whether preceding, following or concomitant; whether essential or happenstantial; potential or extant; etc. For absent such methical distinctions, no well-formed conceptualization is possible.

Most crucially, the absolute or delimited nature of each matter must be determined, with clear recognition of any relevant parameters. For misconstruing an entity by ascribing inappropriate qualities or considering it out of context engenders misconception. Though particulars may be enumerable only to an infinite intellect, one should strive to understand essential general principles. Since generalities intrinsically contain innumerable details, properly grasping a key universal concept enlightens one to the truth of myriads of particulars subsumed within it, suddenly recognizing each one that becomes known through its self-evident belonging to that broader reality. As our sages advise, "One should always have matters of Torah as generalities, not particulars."

Yet general principles must also be properly understood in their full scope and aspects. No detail is truly negligible or unworthy of concern, for nothing exists devoid of consequence at some level. While some specifics may be irrelevant in certain contexts, their impact elsewhere remains significant, given the all-encompassing nature of each general truth that must suffice in every respect. Careful attention and precise tracing of the progression through which each detail flows from prior elements and coalesces into subsequent effects is therefore imperative, that one may gain true wisdom and enlightenment.

Accordingly, dear reader, I have composed this work to elucidate the foundations of faith and service definitively, in a clear systematic manner facilitating authentic comprehension of these pivotal principles in all their aspects, saved from confusion. Herein their roots and branches are bared, interrelations explained, such that they take root and become absorbed within your heart and soul, for the perfection of your mind and being. From this basis, attainment of the knowledge of God throughout Torah, and comprehension of all its hidden treasures, will readily unfold through divine blessing.

I have diligently endeavored to present the ideas in a compelling progression, and language optimally expressive, to impart an accurate picture of these essential ideas I wish to share. Therefore, gentle friend, I ask that you likewise examine this work carefully, hold fast to its guidance, and do not overlook any detail, that no indispensable matter elude you. But delve thoroughly into its words to grasp each concept in its full depth of meaning, that its truths permeate your consciousness, and you find the tranquil clarity for which your soul surely yearns.

This text's title, Derech Hashem, meaning "God and His Ways or The Way of God," reflects its focus: the path of divine truth revealed by the prophets and in the Torah, through which He shapes reality and guides humankind. Correspondingly, this work unfolds in four sections: first, the foundations of existence; second, God's providence; third, prophecy; and fourth, proper service. May each word awaken within you vision and understanding, that you may walk amidst the wonders of His wisdom and ways.

Therefore my brother, who genuinely seek closeness with Hashem, take this as your guide, that God be with you. For He bestows discerning eyes and attentive ears to glimpse the hidden marvels embedded in Torah's every layer of meaning.

Chapter 1 - On the Existence of God

Every Jew must believe and know that there exists a first Being, eternal and everlasting, who brought into existence and continues to bring into existence all that exists, and He is God, blessed be He.

It must also be known that the truth of this Being, blessed be He, is completely beyond grasp by anything other than Him. Only this is known about Him: that He is a perfect Being in all manners of perfection, and absolutely no deficiency exists in Him. These matters we know through tradition from the Patriarchs and Prophets. All of Israel attained them at the event of Mount Sinai and stood firmly upon their truth. They taught them to their children throughout the generations, as Moses our teacher commanded by the mouth of the Almighty—"Lest you forget the things your eyes beheld etc. You shall make them known to your children and grandchildren."[1]

However, all these matters are also proven true by intellectual investigation through conclusive proofs. It will be shown to be necessary that they are so, from the existent beings and their conceptions that we see with our eyes, according to the science of nature, geometry, astronomy, and other sciences. From them will be taken true premises which will yield a demonstration of these true matters. However, we will not elaborate on this now, but only present the premises for their truth. Then, we will arrange the matters clearly, according to the tradition in our possession and what is well known throughout our nation.

It must be known that the existence of this Being, blessed be He, is a necessary existence, that it is completely impossible for Him not to exist.

It must also be known that His existence does not depend on anything else whatsoever; rather, His existence is necessary of itself.

Similarly, it must be known that the existence of God is a simple, unique existence without any composition or multiplicity. All perfection exists within Him in a simple manner. Meaning that as it is for the soul, where are found many varied powers, each of which has its own definition. For example, memory is one power, desire is another power, as is imagination, and none of these enters into the definition of the other at all. The faculty of memory is one definition, and desire is another, and desire does not enter into the definition of memory, nor memory into the definition of desire, and so on for all of them.

However, God, blessed be He, does not possess varied powers, even though in truth there are within Him varied matters—for He indeed desires. He is wise, powerful, and perfect with all perfection. However, the truth of His existence is a singular matter that truly includes within its truth and definition—meaning the truth of its matter—that all perfection is necessarily inherent within it and all deficiencies are necessarily absent from it.

It turns out that all perfection exists within Him not as something added onto His essence and the truth of His matter, but rather due to the truth of His matter itself, which includes all perfection within its truth, for it is impossible for that matter to exist without all perfection inherently.

Behold, in truth, this approach is extremely beyond our grasp and conception. We have virtually no way to explain it nor words to expound it. Our conception and imagination encompass only compound matters bounded by the nature created from Him, for that is what our senses sense and bring the conception of to the intellect.

But in creations, the matters are many and separate. However, we have already prefaced that the truth of His existence is beyond grasp. Nothing can be inferred about the Creator from what is observed in creations, for their matters and existence are not at all equivalent such that we could deduce from one about the other. But this too is from the matters known through tradition, as stated, and proven true through investigation of nature itself, in its laws and dynamics.

For it is certainly impossible that a singular Being found, devoid of all nature's laws, boundaries, and limitations; devoid of any absence or deficiency; of any multiplicity or composition; of any relativity or finite measure; and of any of the attributes of creations. He would be the true cause for all existents and all generated within them. For without this, the existence of these beings we observe and their continuity would have been impossible.

It also must be known that this Being, blessed be He, must necessarily be one and no more. Meaning, it is impossible for multiple existents whose existence is necessary of themselves to exist, but only a singular one must exist with this kind of necessary perfect existence. If any other existents are found, they will only exist because He wills them into existence through His will. All existents would depend on Him and not exist of themselves.

It turns out that these foundational cognitions are six, and they are: the truth of His existence, His perfection, the necessity of His existence, His independence, His simplicity, and His unity.

Chapter 2 - The Purpose of Creation

The purpose of creation is the bestowal of goodness from His own abundance, blessed be He, unto something other than Himself. When you consider this, you realize that He alone, blessed be He, embodies true perfection, completely free from any deficiency. There is no other form of perfection that can compare to His.

Consequently, any form of perfection separate from His is not genuine perfection. It is only termed as perfection in comparison to something that has more flaws. However, absolute perfection is nothing but His own, blessed be He. Thus, His desire to bestow goodness upon another cannot be fulfilled by giving just some goodness; He must give the ultimate good that a creation can receive.

Since He alone is the embodiment of true good, His desire to do good can only be fulfilled by allowing another to partake in that very same inherent good, which is the complete and true good. However, this good is found only in Him. His wisdom, therefore, decreed that the realization of this bestowal should be through providing a space for creations to connect with Him, to the extent of their ability.

This means that although it is impossible for them to attain the same level of perfection as His, by connecting with Him, they can achieve a certain degree of that perfection. They can delight in that true goodness, to the extent that they are capable. Thus, the intention of God in creation is for it to delight in His goodness, to the extent possible.

Nevertheless, His wisdom has determined that for the good to be complete, the recipient of this delight must possess the good themselves. In other words, they must acquire this good on their own, not simply receive it by chance. This resembles, to a certain extent, His own perfection. For He, blessed be He, is inherently perfect, not by chance. Perfection is an intrinsic part of Him, and deficiencies are inherently absent from Him, because of the true nature of His being.

God's wisdom has decreed that for the good to be complete, the one delighting in it must take possession of that good themselves. This means that they must acquire the good through their own efforts, not just stumble upon it. This is a semblance of God's own inherent perfection, not a perfection that just happens to be there. For God is perfect by His very nature, without any deficiencies. His very essence demands perfection and excludes any flaws. However, nothing besides

God can possess this inherent nature. To somewhat resemble Him, a being must at least strive for perfection on their own, not have it imposed upon them, and eliminate any potential deficiencies.

Therefore, God has arranged for both perfection and deficiency to be possible outcomes. He created beings with the potential for both, providing them with the means to attain perfection and eradicate deficiencies on their own. In doing so, they resemble their Creator as closely as possible, making them worthy of connecting with Him and delighting in His goodness.

Furthermore, as these created beings strive for perfection and increasingly resemble their Creator, they also draw closer to Him. This process continues until achieving perfection and being in close connection with Him become one and the same. This is because His existence, blessed be He, is the epitome of true perfection. Therefore, any form of inherent perfection belongs solely to Him, like a branch originates from a root. Although the branch may not reach the original perfection of the root, it is nonetheless an extension and result of that initial perfection.

You can see that true perfection belongs only to His existence, and any deficiency is simply the concealment of His goodness and the hiding of His presence. The revelation of His presence and closeness to Him are the root causes of all perfection. Conversely, the hiding of His presence is the root cause of all deficiencies. The degree of His presence determines the level of perfection, and its absence results in deficiency.

Humanity stands balanced, influenced by the revelation or concealment of God's presence. By actively pursuing perfection and acquiring it through their own efforts, humans grab hold of Him, who is the source of all perfection. The more they perfect themselves, the stronger their connection and closeness to Him become. Eventually, the ultimate achievement of perfection and the ultimate closeness to Him become synonymous, resulting in delight in His goodness and true perfection.

For these dynamics of perfection and deficiency to exist, and for humanity to have the capacity for both as well as the ability to acquire one and remove the other – and for the means towards this perfection to be accessible – there must be a myriad of details in creation. These details are interrelated until the ultimate purpose is fully realized. However, the creation intended for this grand purpose of connection with God is deemed the primary creation. Everything else in existence serves to assist this primary creation in achieving its ultimate purpose.

Specifically, humans represent the true primary creation. All other creations, whether of a higher or lower order, exist solely to aid humanity in fulfilling its complete spiritual purpose in all its varied aspects and requirements. We will delve deeper into this topic later, God willing. For now, understand that wisdom and virtuous character traits are aspects of perfection, meant to refine humanity. Physicality and imagination, on the other hand, are aspects of deficiency, between which humans navigate to achieve their own state of perfection.

The Wisdom of Consciousness – Daat Tevunot

To Understand the Fundamental Principles of Faith

Soul: My desire and will is to settle on some of the things about which it is said (Deuteronomy 4:39), "And you shall know this day and consider it in your heart, that the Lord, He is God," for these are among the fundamentals of our faith which every person is obligated to pursue, to the best of their ability.

Intellect: Where are you heading? The principles are thirteen - on which of them do you wish to contemplate?

Soul: All thirteen principles are validated to me without any doubt; but some are both verified and understood, while others are verified by faith but not clarified through understanding and knowledge.

Intellect: Which are verified to you, and which are clarified to you?

Soul: The existence, unity, eternity, incorporeality and immateriality of God, the creation of the world, prophecy, the prophecy of Moshe, and the Torah from heaven and its eternity - I believe and understand all these without need for further clarification. But providence, reward and punishment, the coming of the Messiah and resurrection of the dead - I believe due to religious obligation, but would like to have a reason to be at ease with them.

Intellect: What difficulties do you have with these matters?
Soul: The great causes overturning in the world that seem to show the opposite of providence, God forbid. Especially since reason cannot see the end and purpose of things, how God leads His creatures, and what is the ultimate aim; for the deeds of the blessed God have such latitude that no heart can contain them. I would like you to teach me a straight path to understand the uprightness of these matters, without turning right or left.

Intellect: There are very difficult and profound issues here, such as the righteous suffering and the wicked prospering, which have troubled even the greatest sages and prophets, including Moshe. They cannot be fully comprehended.

Soul: I will leave the incomprehensible details. But at least provide me with upright general principles, so I may have counsel and reason amidst the latitude of these matters. What my knowledge does not reach, I will accept is not for me to complete.

Intellect: It is certain that the Holy One, blessed be He, established His world on justice and upright, faithful conduct, as the faithful shepherd testified (Deuteronomy 32:4), "The Rock, His work is perfect, for all His ways are justice; a God of faithfulness and without iniquity, just and right is He."
Soul: The uprightness of this justice and depth of this perfect counsel is what I desire to hear explained clearly.

The Purpose of Man's Existence and Service

Intellect: First we must clarify the matter of human existence and the service incumbent upon man, to understand the desired purpose in all this.

Soul: This certainly requires much contemplation to understand clearly in all its parts.

Intellect: The first foundation on which the entire structure stands is that the supreme will wanted man to perfect himself and all creatures for his sake - this itself will be his merit and reward. His merit is that he engages in and labors to attain this perfection, enjoying the fruits of his own efforts. His reward is that he himself will be perfected and delight in goodness forever.

Soul: This foundation includes many angles. I await to hear what you will build upon it, so I may comprehensively discern what it includes. But first, is there a reason why the supreme will wanted this?

Intellect: The reason is simple, and depends on the answer to another question - why did the blessed Creator want to create creatures?

Soul: You answer a matter that is equal for both of us.

Intellect: What we can comprehend is that God, the ultimate good, wanted to create creatures in order to benefit them, for if there are no recipients of good, there is no beneficence. For the beneficence to be complete, He knew in His lofty wisdom that the recipients should receive it through their own efforts, becoming owners of that good without shame, unlike one who receives charity. On this they said (Jerusalem Talmud, Orlah 1:3), "He who eats that which is not his own is ashamed to look at his face."

Soul: The reason settles in my heart. Now complete your words.

Intellect: From this premise emerges a great root to contemplate - the matter of deficiency and its perfection. We need to know what the deficiency is, its consequences, the rectification by which creation is perfected, the way of doing this rectification, and its consequences.

Soul: But I think we first need to understand the perfection man will attain when he has completed his work and rested from his labor. Then we can understand in retrospect all that we have mentioned, for what man ultimately attains is what he initially lacked and needs to strive to acquire.

Intellect: You have spoken correctly. We can now understand perfection in general, not in detail, but this general knowledge will allow us to understand the deficiencies in detail, for every deficiency is the absence of that perfection.

Soul: Say what you have to say about this perfection.

Intellect: This perfection is simple from Scripture and reason; it is that man will cleave to God's holiness and enjoy the perception of His glory without any hindrance or obstruction. As it is written (Isaiah 58:14), "Then you shall delight in the Lord"; (Psalms 140:14), "The upright shall dwell in Your presence"; (Ibid. 16:11), "Fullness of joys in Your presence," and many others like these throughout the words of the prophets and writings, revealed to all nations. In the words of our Sages (Berachot 17a), "The World to Come has no eating or drinking etc., but the righteous sit with their crowns on their heads and delight in the radiance of the Divine Presence."

Reason also dictates this, for the soul is a portion of God above, and its desire is certainly to return and cleave to its source, as is the nature of every effect that yearns for its cause and has no rest until it attains this. But the nature of this cleaving and attainment we do not have the power to understand amidst our current deficiencies. From this we discern that our deficiencies are the distance and hindrance interposing between us and God, making it impossible to cleave to Him as we will after the hindrance passes. This is the deficiency we need to strive to remove from ourselves in order to acquire the perfection we mentioned.

Soul: The reason settles in my heart. Now complete your words.

Intellect: Before proceeding, we must clarify the existence of man and the service incumbent upon him, to understand the desired purpose in all this.

Soul: This matter certainly requires much contemplation to understand it clearly in all its parts.

Intellect: The foundation on which everything stands is that the supreme will wanted man to perfect himself and all that was created for his sake; this will be his merit and reward. His merit - because he is found to be engaged and laboring to attain this perfection; when he attains it - he will enjoy the fruit of his labor and his share of all his toil. His reward - for he will be the perfected one, delighting in goodness forever.

Soul: This foundation includes many facets. I am waiting to hear what you will build upon it, so I may discern in retrospect what is included. But first, is there a reason why the supreme will wanted this?

Intellect: The reason is simple; it depends on the answer to another question: why did the blessed Creator want to create creatures?

Soul: You answer a matter that is equal for both of us.

Intellect: What we can comprehend is that God, may He be blessed, is the ultimate good. It is the law of good to do good; this is what He wanted - to create creatures so that He could benefit them. For if there is no recipient of good, there is no beneficence. For the beneficence to be complete, He knew in His lofty wisdom that it is fitting for the recipients to receive it through their own effort, making them the owners of that good, not remaining with shame in receiving it, like one who receives charity. On this they said (Jerusalem Talmud, Orlah, Chapter 1, Halacha 3), "He who eats that which is not his own is ashamed to look at his face."

Soul: The reason settles in my heart. Now complete your words.

Intellect: From this premise, a great root emerges for us to contemplate: the matter of deficiency and its perfection. We need to know what deficiency is, its consequences, its rectification by which creation will be perfected, the way of doing this rectification, and its consequences.

Soul: I think we first need to understand the perfection that man will attain when he has completed his work and rested from his labor. Then we will understand in retrospect all that we have mentioned. The reason is simple and clear: what man will ultimately attain is what he lacked initially, and because he lacks it, he needs to strive and acquire it.

Intellect: You have spoken correctly. We can now understand perfection in general, not in detail, but by knowing it in general, we will understand the deficiencies in detail in retrospect, for every deficiency is the absence of that perfection.

Soul: Say what you have to say about this perfection.

Intellect: This perfection is simple from Scripture and reason; it is that man will cleave to His holiness, and enjoy the perception of His glory without any hindrance or separating force. As it is written, "Then you shall delight in the Lord"; "The upright shall abide in Your presence"; "In Your presence is fullness of joy," and many others like these, revealed in the words of the prophets and the writings. In the words of our Sages, of blessed memory, "In the World to Come, the righteous sit with their crowns on their heads and delight in the radiance of the Divine Presence." A logical reason: the soul is a portion of God above, and its desire is to return and cleave to its source to comprehend it, as is the nature of every effect that yearns for its cause, having no rest until it attains this. But what this cleaving and comprehension will be - we do not have the power to understand as long as we are in the midst of deficiencies. From this, we discern our deficiencies, for just as perfection is this cleaving, the deficiencies are all the distance and hindrance that interposes between us and Him, making it impossible to cleave to Him as we will after the hindrance passes. This is the deficiency we need to strive to remove to acquire the perfection we mentioned.

Here we need a very fundamental premise.

Soul: What is it?
Intellect: That God, blessed be He, was certainly able to create man and all creation with ultimate perfection; it would have

been fitting for it to be so, for Him being perfect in all kinds of perfection - it is fitting that His deeds should be perfect in all perfection. But when His wisdom decreed to leave man to perfect himself, He created these creatures lacking perfection. This is as if He restrained His attribute of perfection and His great goodness from acting according to the law of His greatness in these creatures, but to make them in the disposition He wanted according to the purpose intended in His lofty thought. Here is included another knowledge, as they said, "Shaddai - that He said to His world 'enough'"; that the heavens were stretching and going until He rebuked them, as written in the Midrash. Certainly, He could have created more and greater creatures than He did; if He had wanted to create His creatures according to the proportion of the Creator, they would have had no measure, just as He and His ability have no measure. But He created them according to the proportion of the created, measuring in them the fitting disposition for them according to what was intended. In any case, He certainly restrained, as it were, His great and infinite ability, so that it would not act in His creatures like its proportion, but according to the proportion of these creatures that are acted upon by it.

Soul: All this is certainly necessary, for it is of the faith that God, may His name be blessed, is omnipotent in all ways; it is impossible to set any limit or measure to His ability. Everything we see that was created from Him in a specific and limited measure - it will not be according to His proportion, God forbid, but according to what His will decreed to act.

Intellect: Let us establish this principle, then proceed to another fundamental premise. This principle: the Master has certainly prevented Himself, as it were, meaning that He prevented His ability in creating His creatures, not making them according to His power, but according to what He wanted and intended for them; He created them lacking so that they themselves would complete themselves, their perfection being their reward in the merit of their efforts to attain it. All this only because He wanted to bestow a complete beneficence.

Soul: Now let us hear this premise that you mentioned.
Intellect: The first premise we need to understand is where man's power is found to perfect his deficiencies, since he was created deficient. We are now entering a very great and wide sea, for we will need many great propositions before coming to complete our subject. You need to be very patient, to understand the matters in proper order, for this is the way of wisdom - to acquire knowledge one after another, until in the end everything will come to light as one complete matter, for which all those premises were needed.

Soul: Speak your words in the proper order, I am listening with all the patience and resolve required.

Intellect: First, you need to know that even though we have said that the blessed Master wanted to give perception of the essence of His perfection to His creatures, it is certainly not the will to give them perception of all His perfection which has no end, limit, or boundary; but on the contrary, only a small edge of it He wanted to reveal to them, in which will be all their delight in attaining it, as we have explained. This is very simple and desirable, for it is impossible for a consequent and created being like us to comprehend all the perfection of the Creator as it is said, "Can you by searching find out God? Can you find out the Almighty unto perfection?" It is found that all that creatures can attain will certainly not be even like a drop from the great sea of the perfection of the Creator, may He be blessed.

Soul: This is simple to all wise of heart, as it has been said, (Psalms 106:2), "Who can express the mighty acts of the Lord," etc.

Intellect: Now, when we consider all the orders of His deeds, all the great deeds He has done since placing man upon the earth, all that He has promised us to do through His holy prophets, what becomes clear to us with absolute clarity is the intensity of His unity. We see that all the other attributes of His perfection which have no end are not clarified to us at all, for we do not have the power to comprehend them. For example, we know that He is wise, but we have not comprehended the end of His wisdom; we know that He knows, but we have not comprehended His knowledge. Therefore they said, (Prayer of Elijah, Tikunei Zohar, Second Introduction), "You are wise, but not with a known wisdom, You are understanding, but not with a known understanding." Since we cannot comprehend these attributes, it follows that we are prohibited from investigating them, for about all such things it is said (Chagigah 13a in the name of Ben Sira 3:21), "You shall not seek what is too wonderful for you, you shall not investigate what is concealed from you"; so they said, (Sefer Yetzirah, Chapter 1), "If your heart runs - return to the place."

But His unity, on the contrary, is revealed and clarified to us with complete clarity. It follows that not only is it clarified to us, but we are obligated to consider this knowledge, to implant it in our hearts with complete resolve without any doubt at all. This is what Moshe our teacher, peace be upon him, commanded us from the mouth of the Almighty (Deuteronomy 4:39), "Know therefore this day, and consider it in your heart, that the Lord He is God in heaven above, and upon the earth beneath; there is none else." The supreme mouth testifies of Himself and informs that all that is gathered from all His great causes with which He overturns in His world, is the revelation of this complete unity; as it is said, (Deuteronomy 32:39), "See now that I, even I, am He, and there is no god with Me," this verse was said after He included the entire cycle of the wheel, which was destined and prepared to revolve in the world, all included in the words of the song of Ha'azinu, as the plain meaning of the verses proves. He sealed the conclusion of His vision with this language, "See now that I, even I, am He," etc. In the words of the prophet Isaiah, it is clarified explicitly (Isaiah 43:10-11), "That you may know and believe Me, understand that I am He; before Me there was no God formed, neither shall any be after Me. I, even I, am the Lord, and beside Me there is no savior"; as it is written (Isaiah 44:6), "I am the first, I am the last, and beside Me there is no God"; as it is written (Isaiah 44:6-7, "That they may know from the rising of the sun, and from the west, that there is none beside Me; I am the Lord, and there is none else; I form the light, and create darkness; I make peace, and create evil; I am the Lord, that does all these things." "That they may know," "that you may know and understand" it is written, implying that He wants us to know with knowledge and understanding. The ultimate of all the success that He promises to Israel is the clarification of His unity to the eyes of all. This matter is mentioned countless times in the words of the prophets, peace be upon them (Isaiah 2:11), "And the Lord alone shall be exalted in that day"; Zechariah 14:9), "And the Lord shall be king... in that day shall the Lord be One, and His name one"; (Zephaniah 3:9), "For then will I turn to the peoples a pure language, that they may all call upon the name of the Lord, to serve Him with one consent." In the end, this is our testimony every day continually (Deuteronomy 6:4), "Hear, O Israel: The Lord our God, the Lord is one."

It is found that all that is truly clarified to us from the intensity of His infinite perfection is only His complete unity. When we look with a contemplative gaze at all the deeds that have been done under the heavens, we see one course that revolves and goes, its rest being only the revelation of this truth. Now we need to understand this unity, what is desired in it, as the verse commanded us, (Deuteronomy 4:39), "and consider it in your heart that the Lord He is God," etc., implying that it requires the resolve of the mind and proper counsel in this matter. I have already said, this is a great and wide sea, in which we have to sail to our heart's content.

MAJOR CONCEPTS OF THE KABBALAH
(From the book: Concepts of the Kabbalah, by Rav R. Afilalo)

Hishtalshelut - Chain of events

In the Kabbalah, the *Hishtalshelut* is the chain of events starting from the first act of G-od in this creation which is the *"Tsimtsum"* (retraction), until the complex arrangements that make the guidance of the worlds. Here, are some of the main concepts of the Kabbalah to better understand this chain of events, and the systems of emanation of the lights and *Sephirot.*

CREATION

Tsimtsum - retraction

Contraction

In the beginning, there was no existence except His presence, the Creator was alone, occupying all space with His light. His light without end, borders or limit, filled everything. He was not bestowing His influence, because there was no one to receive it. When He willed to create, He started to influence. His light being of such holiness and intensity, it is not possible for any being to exist in its proximity.

The *"Tsimtsum (retraction)"* is the first act of the *Ein Sof* (infinite) in the creation. It is the retraction of His light from a certain space and encircling it, so as to reduce its intensity and allow created beings to exist. After this contraction, a ray of His light entered this empty space, and formed the first *Sephirot*

By these boundaries, He revealed the concepts of rigor and limit needed by the created beings, and gave a space for all the created to exist.

'Hallal - vacant space
Space – Vacuum
It is the space left by the *Tsimtsum* (retraction) of His light. This space is circular and contains all possibilities of existence for separated entities, given that they are distanced from the intensity of His light.

Reshimu - imprint

Trace
When His light retracted forming the round space, a trace of it, called the *Reshimu* (imprint) remained inside the *'Hallal* (vacant space). This lower intensity light, allowed a space of existence *(Makom)*, for all the created worlds and beings.
The roots of all future existence and events are in the *Reshimu* (imprint). Nothing can come into existence, without having its root in this imprint.

Kav - ray

Line
A straight ray of light called "*Kav*" (ray), emerged from the *Ein Sof* (infinite), and entered on one side of the "'*Hallal*" (vacant space). The combination of the *Kav* (ray) and the *Reshimu*

(imprint) is what will give existence to the *Sephirot* with which He governs the worlds.

The *Kav* is the innermost interiority of all this creation.

SEPHIROT

Sephira

The light of G-od is unique and of equal force and quality. A *Sephira* is in a way a "filter" which transforms this light in a particular force or attribute, by which the *Ein Sof* (Infinite) directs the worlds.

Each *Sephira* is composed of a vessel called *Keli* (recipient), which holds its part of light called *Or* (light). There is no difference in the *Or* (light) itself; the difference comes from the particularity, or position of the *Sephira*. There are ten *Sephirot,* their names are:

Keter	Crown	**Tiferet**	Beauty
'Hokhma	Wisdom	**Netsa'h**	Glory
Binah	Understanding	**Hod**	Splendor
'Hesed	Bounty	**Yesod**	Foundation
Gevurah	Rigor	**Malkhut**	Kingship

On the right, the *'Hesed* (kindness) *column:* 'Hokhma, 'Hesed, Netsa'h.

In the middle, the *Ra'hamim* (mercy) *column:* Keter, Tiferet, Yesod, Malkhut

On the left, the *Din* (rigor) column: *Binah, Gevurah, Hod.*
There is one more *Sephira* called *Da'at*, which is counted when *Keter* is not, also in the *Ra'hamim* column. There are also configurations of one or more *Sephirot* acting in coordination, which are called *Partsufim* (configurations).

Sephirot Ha'Igulim - circular
Encircling *Sephirot*
After entering the *'Hallal* (vacant space), the *Kav* (ray) made ten circular *Sephirot*, encircling one another, but still maintained a straight shape. These ten *Sephirot* are in charge of the general guidance of the worlds, and are not influenced by the actions of men.

Sephirot HaYashar - straight

Linear *Sephirot*

After making the ten circular *Sephirot*, the *Kav* (ray) maintained his straight shape and made ten other *Sephirot*, but this time in a linear arrangement.

They were later arranged in three columns: right, left and middle, representing the guidance of the world in the manner of *'Hesed, Din* and *Ra'hamim* (Kindness, rigor and mercy). This guidance is dependent on time, and the actions of men.

This first configuration of ten *Sephirot* is called *Adam Kadmon* (Primordial Man).

Adam Kadmon - Primordial man

World on top of *Atsilut* (emanation)

This first configuration, or the first world where the emanated lights were formed into ten *Sephirot* is called *Adam Kadmon* (Primordial Man). It is the union between the *Reshimu* (imprint) and the *Kav* (ray). From this first configuration, all the other worlds came forth into existence. *Adam Kadmon* being at such close proximity to the *Ein Sof* (Infinite), we cannot grasp anything of its nature. Our understanding only starts from the emanations that came out of him in the way of his senses, which are called his branches. From *Adam Kadmon* emerged numerous emanations, four of which are called: sight, hearing, smell and speech, and the four worlds of *Atsilut* (emanation), *Beriah* (creation), *Yetsirah* (formation) and *'Asiah* (action).

Miluyim - spelling

Letters that are added for the spelling of each individual letter of the Name

י-ה-ו-ה

The creative forces or energies are the different powers in the four letters of the name of G-od י-ה-ו-ה, and the various letters added to make their different spellings. Depending on which letters are used, the numerical value of the name changes, and each one of these possibilities becomes different in its nature and actions.

The four *Miluyim* (spellings) are:
- עב ,סג , מה, בן - *'A"V (72), SaG (63), MaH (45), BaN (52)*

יוד הי ויו הי – עב   - *'A"V* = 72
יוד הי ואו הי – סג   - *SaG* = 63
יוד הא ואו הא - מה   - *MaH* = 45
יוד הה וו הה – בן   - *BaN* = 52

Each name can also be divided and subdivided as:
'A"V of 'A"V, SaG of 'A"V, MaH of 'A"V ...
BaN of BaN of SaG, SaG of MaH of 'A"V etc.

Sephirot of BaN (52)

From the eyes of *Adam Kadmon* (Primordial man) came out ten *Sephirot* of the aspect of the name of *BaN (52)*. They correspond to the feminine aspect - rigor, and are the root of deterioration. When they came out, the first three *Sephirot* – KHB (Keter, 'Hokhma, Binah), were able to stand in three columns. The seven lower *Sephirot* could not stand in this order; they formed a single descending line and broke. This imperfect arrangement is the first origin of the *Sitra A'hra* or "evil".

*Shv*irat HaKelim - Breaking of the vessels

The *Sephirot* of *Keter*, *'Hokhma* and *Binah* of *BaN (52)* that came out from the eyes of *Adam Kadmon* (Primordial man), received and contained their lights because they were in the three-column arrangement. The seven lower *Sephirot* could not contain their lights and broke. Their *Kelim* (recipients) descended to the world of *Beriah* (creation). Their lights also fell, but stayed in *Atsilut* (emanation).

The roots of all the created are in the seven lower *Sephirot*, the three first *Sephirot* are like a crown on them to repair and direct them. In the first three *Sephirot* there is not really a notion of damage, they are above men's deeds, and are not affected by their sins.

This deficient state caused a fall not only of these *Sephirot*, but of all the worlds also.

Rapa'h Nitsutsot - 288 Sparks

To sustain the *Kelim* (recipients) after they broke, 288 sparks of the lights came down as well, because a connection to their original lights was needed to keep them alive. The fall of the *Kelim* (recipients), is also called their death. It is important to understand that all that happens in our world is similar to what occurred in this fall.

The goal of all the works, deeds and prayers of men in this existence, is to help and participate in the ascent of these sparks to their origin. At the completion of this *Tikun* of unification between the fallen sparks and their *Keli* (recipient), it will be the time of the resurrection of the dead and the arrival of *Moshia'h*.

Sephirot of MaH (45)

After the breaking of the *Kelim* (recipients) and the separation from their lights, it was necessary for the guidance of the world that reparation be done. From the forehead of *Adam Kadmon* (Primordial man) came out ten *Sephirot* of the aspect of the name of *MaH (45);* corresponding to the masculine - reparation. In contrast to the *Sephirot* of *BaN (52) which* correspond to the feminine aspect - rigor, and are the root of deterioration.

The *Tikun* (rectification) was done by the union of the *Sephirot* of *MaH (45)* (mercy) and *BaN (52)* (rigor) in complex arrangements, as to allow the feminine *BaN* to be repaired by the masculine *MaH,* and for the *Sephirot* to stand in the three-column arrangement of kindness, rigor and mercy. With the proper order of the *Sephirot* in place, various configurations that are called *Partsufim* completed the creation.

PARTSUFIM – Configurations

Partsuf

A *Partsuf* is a configuration of one or more *Sephirot* acting in coordination.

There are five main *Partsufim* (configurations):
- *Arikh Anpin*
- *Abah*
- *Imah*
- *Zeir Anpin*
- *Nukvah*

And one on top of them; *'Atik Yomin* (clothed inside *Arikh Anpin*).

From these five *Partsufim* (configurations); emerge seven more. They emanate from the ten *Sephirot* as follows:

From *Keter:*
- *'Atik Yomin* and his *Nukvah*
- *Arikh Anpin* and his *Nukvah*

From *'Hokhma: - Abah*
- From *Malkhut* of *Abah - Israel Saba*
- From *Malkhut* of *Israel Saba - Israel Saba* 2

From *Binah: - Imah*
- From *Malkhut* of *Imah -Tevunah*
- From *Malkhut* of *Tevunah - Tevunah* 2

Israel Saba and *Tevunah* are also called by their initials *ISOT* or *ISOT* 2.

From *'Hesed, Gevurah, Tiferet, Netsa'h, Hod, and Yesod:* - *Zeir Anpin*.

From *Zeir Anpin:* - *Ya'acov, Israel*.

From *Malkhut:* - *Nukvah*, divided in two *Partsufim* (configurations): *Ra'hel* and *Leah*

The *Partsufim Zeir Anpin* and *Nukvah* are the root of all the created. It is by their *Tikunim* (actions) that the guidance of justice is manifested. Here, the "*Tikun*" is a description of the actions, illuminations and inter-relations of the *Sephirot* and *Partsufim*. These *Tikunim* will result in various illuminations of different intensities, for the guidance of the worlds.

Partsuf 'Atik Yomin

The *Partsuf 'Atik* is superior to all the *Partsufim* (configurations). His *Nukvah* (feminine) is never separated from him, her back attached to his back. *Partsuf 'Atik* makes the connection between each world.

Partsuf Arikh Anpin

The innermost of all the other *Partsufim* (configurations) is *Arikh Anpin* and his *Nukvah*, they make one *Partsuf*; the masculine on the right, and the feminine on the left. *Arikh Anpin* is the first *Partsuf* in *Atsilut* (emanation), and the root of all the others which are his branches.

Partsufim (configurations) Abah and Imah

These two *Partsufim* are the link between the superior *Partsuf Arikh Anpin* and *Z'uN (Zeir Anpin and Nukvah)*. *Abah* is the *Sephira 'Hokhma, Imah* is the *Sephira Binah*.

Partsuf Zeir Anpin

Zeir Anpin (Z"A) is composed of the six lower *Sephirot:* *'Hesed, Gevurah, Tiferet, Netsa'h, Hod, Yesod.*

The abundance comes down to the world when *Zeir Anpin* and *Nukvah (Z"uN)* unite. It is given to *Nukvah,* and from her, to the lower worlds. All this abundance that comes down to the world, proceeds from the various *Zivugim* (unions) of *Z"uN.* Each new day, is of a new emanation that governs it. For each day, there are new *Zivugim* of different aspects of *Z"uN.*

The guidance of the world is dependent on the different positioning and interaction, of *Z"A* and *Nukvah,* since they have a direct effect on the measures and balance of the factors of kindness, rigor and mercy.

The goal of the service of the creatures, is to help prepare the *Partsufim* (configurations) *Z"A* and *Nukvah* for the *Zivug* (union), and this by the elevation and adhesion of the worlds by way of the *Tefilot* (prayers) and *Mitsvot* (commandments).

Partsuf Nukvah

The *Partsuf Nukvah* represents the feminine – the principle of receiving. It comprises of two distinct *Partsufim*: *Ra'hel and Leah*.

The *Partsufim* (configurations) of *Zeir Anpin* and *Nukvah* are the root of all the created. It is by them, that the guidance of justice is manifested. There is perfection for the masculine only when it completes itself with its feminine.

Mo'hin - brains

The *Mo'hin* (brains) are the directive force given to the *Partsuf*. There are interior and encircling *Mo'hin*.

Zivugim - Unions

The *Zivug* is the union of the masculine with its feminine. All the outcomes of the higher emanations are a result of the different unions of the masculine and feminine lights.

There are different kinds of *Zivugim*:
- the ones for the construction of the worlds
- for the building of the *Partsufim* (configurations),
- for the guidance of the worlds.

For the abundance to come down to the world, *Zeir Anpin* needs to unite with *Nukvah*. There can be abundance only when the masculine and the feminine are in harmony. Each day, according to the actions of man, the *Tefilot* (prayers) during the week, *Shabbat* or holidays, and depending on time, various configurations allow different *Zivugim*, and therefore outflows of abundance of variable intensities.

The guidance of the world is dependent on the different positioning and interaction, of these masculine and feminine *Partsufim.* The results of these unions vary, and produce different emanations of kindness, rigor and mercy.

The goal of the service of the creatures, is to help prepare the *Partsufim* (configurations) *Z"A* and *Nukvah* for the *Zivug* (union), and this, by the elevation and adhesion of the worlds by way of the *Tefilot* and *Mitsvot*.

THE FOUR WORLDS

Atsilut - emanation

First world

There are four worlds. The first to unfold from *Adam Kadmon* (Primordial man) is called *Atsilut;* the world of emanation, where there is no existence of the separated, and no *Sitra A'hra* (negative force) even at its lowest levels. It is the first of the four worlds, on top of *Beriah* (creation), *Yetsirah* (formation) and *'Asiah* (action). From *Atsilut* (emanation) unfolded all the lower worlds, which are the source of existence for the physical worlds, and the possibility of reward, punishment and evil.

Beriah - creation

World of the souls

The second world is *Beriah* (creation); the world of the *Neshamot*; of the souls.

Yetsirah - formation

World of the angels
The third world is *Yetsirah* (formation); the world of formation, the world of the angels.

'Asiah - action

 World of physical existence
'Asiah (action) is the fourth world; the world of action, the world of physical existence. The three superior worlds of *Atsilut* (emanation), *Beriah* (creation) and *Yetsirah* (formation), are interior to the fourth world of *'Asiah* (action).

From the last level of the *Sephirot* of *'Asiah* - *Malkhut* of *'Asiah*, the *Sitra A'hra* came out.

Tikunim - Reparation or action

In Hebrew, the word "*Tikun*" has different meanings. It can be understood as reparation or rectification, and also as function, relation or action.

There are different types of *Tikunim:*
- *Tikunim* that took place in the first emanations to repair the worlds
- *Tikunim* for the construction and inter-relations of the *Sephirot* and *Partsufim* (configurations)

- *Tikunim* of certain *Partsufim* (function or action) for the guidance of the worlds
- *Tikunim* (rectifications) for the *Neshamot*.

For the guidance, the *Tikunim* of the *Partsufim* (configurations) are the actions, illuminations and inter-relations of the *Sephirot* and *Partsufim,* and their influence on the worlds. These *Tikunim* result in various illuminations of different intensities, depending on time and the actions of man.

The *Tikun* of the soul is realized by the *Gilgul* (reincarnation), and by the *'Ibur* (attachment).

By giving man a role in the general *Tikun (Tikun 'Olam),* it is now up to him to restore, and make the necessary reparations to the world. However, if man does not act accordingly, the *Tikun* will still be realized, but in the time set by the Creator.

Hanhagua - Guidance

The Kabbalah is the only science that explains to us in the least details, the true guidance of the world, so that we may understand His will. It teaches us that the world is guided by an extremely complex system of forces or lights, which through their interactions provoke chain reactions that impact directly on man and the guidance of the worlds. Each one of these reactions has numerous ramifications with many details and results.

The guidance of the worlds is done through the influence of the different *Sephirot* and *Partsufim* (configurations).

There are two main kinds of guidance:
- The general guidance, which is for the subsistence of the worlds, and is not influenced by the actions of men. This guidance is by the encircling *Sephirot*.

- The variable guidance, which is on the basis of justice, reward and punishment, and is dependant on the actions of men. This guidance is by the linear *Sephirot*.

The guidance of the world is dependent on the different positioning and interactions of the masculine and feminine *Partsufim*, since they have a direct effect on the measure and balance of the factors of kindness, rigor and mercy. The masculine *Partsufim* bestow kindness, the feminine bestow rigor. By their unions, different equilibriums of the two forces of kindness and rigor make the guidance.

Ratson Lehashpia' - Will to bestow

The will of the Creator is to bestow goodness on His creatures, all the levels of creation were put in place so His kindness could emanate to them, yet in such a way that they would be able to receive it.

Ratson Lekabel - Desire to receive

By his nature man is himself a *Keli* (recipient) with a will to receive without limits, and containing a spiritual light; his soul. A guidance based on this desire will permit anything without restriction, and not allow man to have merit.

The perfect goal for man is to elevate his bodily desires by sanctifying his ways, and resemble his Creator by becoming a giver with a will to bestow goodness to all.

Giluy Yi'hudo - Revelation of his unity
The goal of all these possibilities of guidance have only one purpose: to allow man to merit by his own efforts, to get closer to his Creator, receive His goodness, and live the *Dvekut* – the adhesion with G-od. In this way, man will attain perfection and be directly involved in the ultimate goal of the creation, which is the revelation of G-od's Sovereignty – *Giluy Ye'hudo.*

176

Glossary of Kabbalah

א"ק
A"K
Adam Kadmon
Initials

אבא
Abah
Partsuf Abah
One of the five main *Partsufim* (configurations)
 It is the *Sephira 'Hokhma*

אבא ואמא
Abah ve Imah
Partsufim Abah and Imah
These two *Partsufim (configurations)* are essential for the guidance of the worlds, *Abah* is the *Sephira 'Hokhma, Imah* is the *Sephira Binah*

אבחנה
Av'hana
Distinction – Insight
Understanding of the deeper meaning or Kabbalistic interpretation

אבר
Ever
Organ – Limb (Anthropomorphism)
In the language of Kabbalah, anthropomorphisms are used only to illustrate the esoteric power of these forces

אדם קדמון
Adam Kadmon
Primordial man - World on top of Atsilut
This first configuration, or the first world where the
emanated lights were formed into ten *Sephirot*

אדנ- י
Adona-y
Adona-y
One of the names of G-od, represented by the
Sephira Malkhut

אהי-ה
AHY-H
One of the names of G-od, represented by the
Sephira Keter

אור
Or
Light
Term used to describe an emanation, a force or energy

אחור
A'hor
Backside – Behind
In general it represents rigor

אחר
A'her
Other
Name also used for the other side or negative force

אילן
Ilan
Tree
The disposition of the *Sephirot* in the three
pillars arrangement is called the *Sephirotic* tree

אין סוף
Ein Sof
The without end or limit - Infinite
One of the names of G-od
The Name of G-od that is the most used in the Kabbalah

אלוה-ים
Elohi-m
One of the names of G-od, represented by the
Sephira Gevurah
 In general it denotes rigor in the actions of G-od

אמא
Imah
Partsuf Imah
One of the five main configurations
 It is the *Sephira Binah*

אצילות
Atsilut
World of Emanation
It is the highest of the four worlds, on top of the worlds of
Beriah, Yetsirah and *'Asiah*
From *Atsilut* unfolded all the lower worlds, which are the
source of existence for the physical worlds

אצילות בריאה יצירה עשייה
Atsilut, Beriah, Yetsirah and 'Asiah
From the first configuration; *Adam Kadmon* (*Primordial man*) emanations made the four lower worlds
The first world is *Atsilut* – the world of emanation
 Under the divider of *Atsilut* is the world of *Beriah* (creation) - the world of the *Neshamot* (souls)
 Under the divider of *Beriah* is the world of *Yetsirah* (formation) - the world of the angels
 Under the divider of *Yetsirah* is the world of *'Asiah* (action) - the physical world

אריז"ל
Ari Z'al
Rabbi Its'hak Luria Ashkenazi
Born in Jerusalem in 1534, died in 1572 in Tsfat, Israel
He was the leading Kabbalist in Tsfat, he explained and clarified all the main concepts of the Kabbalah
 He is the author of the "Ets 'Haim"

אריך אנפין
Arikh Anpin
Partsuf – Long countenance
It is the main *Partsuf* (configuration) in each world
 All the other *Partsufim* are his "branches"

אתב"ש
ATBaSH
Permutation of letters to understand hidden meanings of words
 First letter replaced by the last, second by the before last etc

ב"ן
BaN (52)
Miluy (spelling) of the name with a total of 52 ה-ו-ה-י
It corresponds to the feminine aspect - rigor

בינה
Binah
Sephira (understanding)
Third of the *Sephirot*
ברוך הוא
Barukh Hu, or B'H
Blessed He is
Used after the pronunciation or writing of G-od's names

בריאה
Beriah
World of creation – of the souls
The second world to unfold is called *Beriah*; the world of creation
 It is the world of the *Neshamot* (souls)
 It is under *Atsilut* and on top of *Yetsirah* and *'Asiah*

בר יוחאי
Bar Yo'hay
Rabbi Shim'on Bar Yo'hay
To escape the Romans he went into hiding with his son Rabbi El'azar in a cave for thirteen years and composed the Zohar

ברכה
Berakhah
Blessing
When saying the blessing with the Kabbalistic meditation on the appropriate words or names, we act

and participate directly on the *Tikun* (repair) of the thing being blessed

ג' ראשונות
Shalosh Rishonot
The three first Sephirot
Keter, 'Hokhma, Binah

ג"ר
G"aR
The three first Sephirot
Keter, 'Hokhma, Binah

גבול
Gevul
Boundary – Limit
By putting boundaries to His light, the Creator revealed the concepts of rigor and limit needed by the created beings, and gave a space for all the created to exist

גבורה
Gevurah
Rigor
One of these manifestations of this light once filtered by the *Sephira Gevurah* emanates rigor
Rigor is mostly manifested by all the feminine aspects as: the name of *BaN (52)*, the *Sephira Gevurah* and by all the concealments of the masculine aspects which represent bounty

גבורה
Gevurah
Sephira (Rigor)
Fifth of the *Sephirot*

גימטריה
Gematria
Numerical values of the letters
Each letter has its own numerical value
The fact that some words have the same numerical value
is not just coincidence, but denotes a similarity or
complementarity

גלגול
Gilgul
Reincarnation
The *Tikun* of the soul is realized by the
Gilgul (reincarnation), and by the *'Ibur* (attachment)
 The *Gilgul* is the reincarnation of a soul from the time of
birth until death

גן עדן
Gan 'Eden
The Garden of Eden
The place of rest for the *Neshamot* (souls) after their
separation with their former physical bodies
 There is a lower and a higher *Gan 'Eden*

גן עדן עליון
Gan 'Eden 'Elyon
The upper Garden of Eden
In the higher *Gan 'Eden*, the *Neshamot* (souls) are
enjoying pure spiritual pleasures, and do not have any
spiritual image resembling their former bodies

גן עדן תחתון
Gan' Eden Takhton
The lower Garden of Eden

In the lower *Gan 'Eden*, the *Neshamot* (souls) are enjoying spiritual pleasures but still have a spiritual body resembling their former bodies

גשמיות
Gashmiut
Corporeality
The possibilities of existence for separated entities became possible, only once distanced from the intensity of His light
 The greater the distance more is the corporality possible

דו"ן
D"uN
Masculine and feminine
Initials

דוכרין ונוקבין
Dukhrin Ve Nukvin
Masculine and feminine

דומם, צומח, חי, מדבר
Domem, Tsomeakh, 'Hay, Medaber
Mineral, vegetal, animal and the spoken
In parallel to the four worlds of *Atsilut, Beriah, Yetsirah* and *'Asiah,* there are four types of existence in our world: mineral and), חי(animal), צומח(vegetal), דומם) מדבר)(the speaking

דעת
Da'at
Sephira (Knowledge)
Fourth of the *Sephirot*

דעת
Da'at
Knowledge
The essential knowledge is the one of the will of the
Creator and His ways of guidance in this existence, as
explained in the Kabbalah

הארה
Hearah
Illumination
Special outburst of a light for a specific purpose

הוד
Hod
Sephira – Glory
Eighth of the *Sephirot*

הוי"ה
HaVaYaH
One of the ways of mentioning the Tetragamon
□ without pronouncing it י-ה-ו-ה

היכל
Hekhal
Portal – Level
The *Hekhalot* are the different levels of ascension of the
Tefilot before reaching the *'Olam Atsilut* during the
Amidah

הנהגה
Hanhagah
Guidance
The guidance of the worlds is done through the
influence of the different *Sephirot* and *Partsufim*
(configurations)

הרחקה
Har'hakah
Distancing
Distance denotes a contrary or a non compatibility
The possibilities of existence for separated entities
became possible, only once distanced from the intensity
of His light

השגה
Hasagah
Attainment - Comprehension
To reach a higher level of understanding or
comprehension, one has to make the effort of studying
the *Sod* (secret) of the Torah which is the Kabbalah

השתלשלות
Hishtalshelut
Evolution - Chain of events
In the Kabbalah the *Hishtalshelut* is the chain of events
starting from the first act of G-od in this creation which is
the "*Tsimtsum*" *(retraction)*, until the complex
arrangements that make the guidance of the worlds

ז' מלכים
Sheva' Malkhin
Seven kings
The seven kings of Edom that died (Bereshit, 36, 31),
correspond to the seven lower *Sephirot* that broke during
the *Shvirat HaKelim* (breaking of the vessels)

ז"א
Z"A
Zeir Anpin (Small countenance)
Initials of *Partsuf Zeir Anpin*, used more often than the full
name

ז"ת
Za"T
Zain Takhtonot
Initials of the seven lower *Sephirot*

זו"ן
Z"UN
Zeir Anpin and Nukvah
Initials of *Partsuf Zeir Anpin and Nukvah,* used more often than the full names

זוהר
Zohar
The book of splendor, written by Rabbi Shim'on Bar Yo'hay
The *Zohar* is the esoteric and mystical explanation of the Torah, and the base for most of the Kabbalah writings

זיו
Ziv
Radiance – Illumination
A superior light will illuminate to a lower one to influence it, or to create a new emanation

זיווג
Zivug
Union
The *Zivug* is the union of the masculine with its feminine
 All the outcomes of the higher emanations are a result of the different unions of the masculine and feminine lights

זין תחתונות
Zayin Takhtonot
Seven lower
The seven lower *Sephirot:*

'Hesed, Gevurah, Tiferet, Netsa'h, Hod, Yesod, Malkhut

זכר
Zakhar
Masculine
There are masculine *Partsufim* that bestow kindness, and feminine *Partsufim* that bestow rigor
 By their union, different equilibriums of these two forces (kindness and rigor), make the guidance

זעיר אנפין
Zeir Anpin
Partsuf Zeir Anpin (Small countenance)
Zeir Anpin (Z"A) is composed of the seven lower *Sephirot: 'Hesed, Gevurah, Tiferet, Netsa'h, Hod, Yesod* and *Malkhut* of a world

חבד
'HaBaD
'Hokhma, Binah and Da'at
Initials of the first triplet of the *Sephirot: 'Hokhma, Binah and Da'at*

חגת
'HaGaT
'Hesed, Gevurah and Tiferet
Initials of the second triplet of the *Sephirot: 'Hesed, Gevurah and Tiferet*

חוץ
'Huts
Outside
Denotes a position of non-compatibility or a contrary

חיבור
'Hibur
Attachment
All the *Sephirot* and *Partsufim* have a certain degree of attachment between them

חיה
'Hayah
Fourth level of the soul
'Hayah is the fourth level and can only be acquired after the preceding levels

חיות
'Hayut
Livelihood
The livelihood of everything, whether positive or negative has only one origin; G-od the Creator and sustainer of all

חיצוניות
'Hitsoniut
Exteriority (The)
The external or negative force – *Sitra A'hra* is also called exteriority

חכמה
'Hokhma
Sephira – Wisdom
Second of the *Sephirot*

חכמת האמת
'Hokhmat HaEmet
Knowledge of the truth
One of the names of the Kabbalah

חלל
'Hallal
Space – Vacuum
The space left by the *Tsimtsum* (retraction) of His light

חסד
'Hesed
Bounty - Kindness
Kindness is manifested by the different positioning and
interaction of the masculine and feminine *Partsufim*

חסד
'Hesed
Sephira (Bounty)
Fourth of the *Sephirot*

חסד, גבורה, תפארת
'Hesed, Gevurah and Tiferet
Second triplet of the *Sephirof*

טמא
Tameh
Impure
State of distance from the *Kedushah* and closeness to the
Sitra A'hra (negative force)

י -ה ו ה
Adona-y
Y-H-V-H *Tetragamon* (ה-ו-ה-י)
Main name of G-od, reveals kindness and mercy,
represented by the *Sephira Tiferet*
The creative forces or energies are the different powers in
the letters of the name of G-od and the various, ה-ו-ה-י
letters added to make their different spellings

יום
Yom
Day
Each new day, is of a new emanation that governs it

יחוד
Yi'hud
Unification – Union
The union of the *Sephirot* or *Partsufim* for the *Zivug* and for the descent of the abundance

יחודו
Yi'hudo
His unicity
The light of G-od is unique, of equal force, quality and beyond all description

יחידה
Ye'hidah
Fifth level of the soul
Ye'hidah is the fifth level and can only be acquired after the preceding levels

יסוד
Yesod
Sephira (Foundation)
Ninth of the *Sephirot*

יצירה
Yetsirah
World of formation – of the angels
The third world to unfold is called *Yetsirah*; the world of formation, the world of the angels
 It is under *Atsilut* and *Beriah* and on top of *'Asiah*

יצר
Yetser
Instinct – Impulse
The *Yetser Hatov* corresponds to the good or positive impulse in man, the *Yetser Hara'* is his bad or negative impulse

ירושלים
Yerushalaim
Jerusalem
The closest place to G-od's emanations

ישסו"ת
ISOT
Partsufim Israel Saba and Tevunah
Initials

כוונה
Kavanah
Intention – Concentration
Kavanah is to understand the words, and concentrate on the intention of the blessing or the *Tefilah* (prayer)

כחב
Ka'HaB
Keter, 'Hokhma, Binah
Initials

כיסא
Kisey
Throne
There are three main types of thrones:
Kisey HaDin - throne of justice
Kisey Hakavod - throne of glory
Kisey Ra'hamim - throne of mercy

כלי
Keli
Recipient –Vessel
Each *Sephira* is composed of a vessel called *Keli*, which holds its part of light called *Or*

כתר
Keter
Sephira – Crown
First and most important of the *Sephirot*

כתר, חכמה, בינה
Keter, 'Hokhma, Binah
The three first *Sephirot*, often referred as the *Ga'R*; *Shalosh Rishonot* (the three first ones)

לאה
Leah
Leah - Partsuf Nukvah
The *Partsuf Nukvah* comprises of two distinct *Partsufim* (configurations)*: Ra'hel* and *Leah, Partsuf Leah* of the aspect of rigor

להחמיר
LeHa'hmir
To be more stringent
A strict observance of all the details when accomplishing a *Mitsva* or *Tefilah*

לקבל
Lekabel
To receive
The word Kabbalah comes from the verb *Lekabel* (to receive), but to receive it is first necessary to want, and to

become a *Keli* (recipient) able to receive and contain this knowledge

מ"ה
MaH (45)
Miluy (spelling) of the name with a total of 45 י-ה-ו-ה
The name of *MaH (45)* is the *Miluyim* (spelling) of , א
 (Vav) line in the middle (mercy) that unites) ו(which is a
two (Yud) (kindness and rigor) י
 It is of a masculine aspect and represents mercy

מ"ן
M"N
Mayin Nukvin (feminine waters)
Initials

מוחין
Mo'hin
Brains
The *Mo'hin* are the directive force given to the *Partsuf* (configuration)

מיין דוכרין
Mayin Dukhrin
Masculine waters
One of two emanations allegorically called masculine waters

מיין נוקבין
Mayin Nukvin
Feminine waters
One of two emanations allegorically called feminine waters

מילוי
Miluy
Spelling
Depending on which letters are used, the numerical value of a name changes, and each one of these possibilities becomes different in its nature and actions

מלאכים
Malakhim
Angels
The world of the angels is the third world; *'Olam Yetsirah -* the world of formation

מלכות
Malkhut

Sephira (Royalty)
Tenth of the *Sephirot*

מעשה בראשית
Ma'ase Bereshit
Works or acts of the creation
Name given for all the details of the beginning of the creation, from the *Tsimtsum*, the first worlds, the *Sephirot* etc

מעשה המרקבה
Ma'ase Hamerkava
Works or acts of the Heavenly Chariot
Name given for all the details of the *Sephirot, Partsufim, Tikunim* and *Zivugim* that make the guidance

מצוה
Mitsva
Commandment

As there are 613 *Mitsvot,* there are 613 veins and bones to man, 613 parts to the soul, and each *Sephira* and *Partsuf* also has 613 parts
This number is not arbitrary as there are important interrelations and interactions between them

מקובל
Mekubal
Kabbalist - Accepted
A *Mekubal* is a person who is accepted to receive this knowledge, and is able to hold it by living in the path of Torah and rightness to strengthen himself constantly

מקום
Makom
Place – space
Until the world was created, He and His Name were One
 He willed to create, and contracted His light to create all beings by giving them a space

מקור
Makor
Source – Origin
Each emanation has its source in the higher realms

מרקבה
Merkavah
Heavenly chariot
The *Partsufim* (configurations), *Sephirot* and the *Sephirot* tree, with all their inter-relations, actions and illuminations

משל
Mashal
Allegory
Sometimes used to explain or illustrate difficult concepts

מתלבש
Mitlabesh
Dress
Partsufim dress on, or in, each other
The more important *Partsuf* will dress inside the less
important to direct him

נהי
NeHY
Netsa'h, Hod and Yesod
Initials of the third triplet of the *Sephirot: Netsa'h, Hod and
Yesod*

נוטריקון
Notrikun (acronym)
Notrikun is a method of interpretation in which initials of
different words make a new word
אמן = אל מלך נאמן

נוקבא
Nukvah
Feminine - Sephira Malkhut – Partsuf Ra'hel, Leah
The *Partsuf* (configuration) *Nukvah* represents the
feminine – the principle of receiving, It comprises of two
distinct *Partsufim: Ra'hel* and *Leah*

ניצוצות
Nitsutsot
Sparks
To sustain the *Kelim* after they broke, 288 sparks of their
lights came down as well, because a connection to their
original lights was needed to keep them alive

נפש
Nefesh
Soul - First level of the soul
Nefesh is the first level and lower level of the soul

נפש, רוח, נשמה, חיה, יחידה
Nefesh, Rua'h, Neshama, 'Hayah and Ye'hidah
The soul has five names: *Nefesh, Rua'h, Neshama, 'Hayah* and *Ye'hidah*, which correspond to its five levels
The soul is the spiritual entity inside the body, the latter being only his outer garment

נצח
Netsa'h
Sephira (splendor)
Seventh of the *Sephirot*

נקבה
Nekevah
Female – Feminine
Rigor is manifested by all the feminine aspects and by the concealment of the masculine aspects, which represent bounty

נקודות
Nekudot
Punctuation – Vowels – Points
Each vowel corresponds to a *Sephira*
It in a way translates, with the combination of the letters, the inner identity of the word

נר"ן
NaRaN
Nefesh, Rua'h, Neshama
Initials of the first three levels of the souls

נשמה
Neshama
Soul - Third level of the soul
Neshama is the third level and can be acquired only after acquiring the level of *Nefesh* and *Rua'h*

ס"ג
SaG (63)
Miluy (spelling) of the name with a total of 63 י-ה-ו-ה
The name of *SaG* is the second level of the four names for a total of 63

ס"מ
S"M
Initials of the main destructive Angel

סגולה
Segulah
Remedy – Protection
Names, or combinations of names of angels with special signs or incantations, written on parchment to protect, or to invoke particular powers

סודות - סוד
Sod - ot
Secret -s
Through the knowledge of Kabbalah, we can get to a level of true understanding of the will of the Creator, and in a way "decode" the profound secrets of our holy Torah

סיטרא אחרא
Sitra A'hra
Negative force
The root of the *Sitra A'hra* is in the lack, or absence of the *Kedushah*

ספירה
Sephira
The light of G-od is unique and of equal force and quality
A *Sephira* is in a way a "filter" which transforms this light
in a particular force or attribute, by which the Creator
guides the worlds

ספירות
Sephirot
Plural of Sephira
See Sephira

ספירות הישר
Sephirot HaYashar
Straight Sephirot
Sephirot arranged in three columns: right, left and middle,
representing the guidance of the world in the manner of
'Hesed, Din and *Ra'hamim* (Kindness, rigor and mercy)

ספירות העיגולים
Sephirot Ha'Igulim
Encircling Sephirot
These ten *Sephirot* are in charge of the general
guidance of the worlds, and are not influenced by the
actions of men

ע"ב
'A"V
Miluy (spelling) of the name with a total of 72 י-ה-ו-ה
The name of *'A"V* is of the highest level of the four names
of *'A"V, SaG, MaH (45)* and *BaN (52)*

עב, סג מה, בן
'A"V, SaG, MaH, BaN
Spellings of the Name ה-ו-ה-י
'A"V (72), SaG (63), MaH (45), BaN (52)
The creative forces or energies are the different powers in
the four letters of the name of G-od
  and the various letters added to make their ה-ו-ה-י,
different spellings

עבודה
'Avodah
Service – Duty
One of the main goals of all the works, deeds and prayers
of men in this existence, is to help and participate in the
ascent of the fallen 288 sparks to their origin

עולם
'Olam
World
A 'Olam is a possibility and a type of existence, in a
particular dimension

עשיה
'Asiah
World of action – of man
The fourth world to unfold is called 'Asiah - action, the
world of physical existence

עשר
'Eser
Ten
Number of Sephirot in each world, in each Sephira,
Partsuf or configuration

עת
'Et
Time – Moment
Each moment can be described in term of permutation of
the names of G-od, and by the various *Sephirot and
Partsufim*

עתיק יומין
'Atik Yomin
Partsuf – Ancient
The *Partsuf 'Atik* is superior to all the *Partsufim*

פנימיות
Pnimiut
Internality
What is inside or interior
 Also applies to deeper meaning or spirituality

פרצוף
Partsuf
Configuration - Countenance
A *Partsuf* is a configuration of one or more
Sephirot acting in coordination

פרצופים
Partsufim
Configurations
See Partsuf

צדיק
Tsadik
Righteous
State of outmost closeness to the *Kedushah* and distance
from the *Sitra A'hra (negative force)*
Also attributed to the *Sephira Yesod*

צינור
Tsinor
Conduit
A *Sephira* is in a way a "conduit" which transforms the light in a particular force or quality, by which the Creator guides the worlds

צל"ם
Tselem
Mo'hin (brains) of Z"A
The *Tselem* are the directive force - *Mo'hin* (brains) given to *Z"A*

צמצום
Tsimtsum
Contraction - Retraction
The "*Tsimtsum*" is the first act of the *Ein Sof* (Infinite) in the creation
It is the retraction of His light from a certain space and encircling it, so as to reduce its intensity and allow created beings to exist

קבלה
Kabbalah
The Kabbalah is the mystical and esoteric explanation of the Torah
 It teaches the unfolding of the worlds, the various ways of guidance of these worlds, the role of man in the creation, the will of the Creator and so on

קבלה מעשית
Kabbalah Ma'asit
Practical Kabbalah
The "other" type of Kabbalah, where names or combinations of names of angels are used with special

signs or incantations, sometimes written on parchment, to invoke particular powers and alterate normal states of events

קדוש
Kadosh
Holly – Saintly
State of closeness to the *Kedushah* and distance from the *Sitra A'hra* (negative force)

קדוש ברוך הוא
Kadosh Barukh Hu
Saintly and Blessed He is
One of the names of G-od

קדושה
Kedushah
Sanctity – Holiness
By accomplishing the *Mitsvot* and the *Tefilot* (prayers), men do the *Tikunim* (rectifications) necessary to detach the *Klipot* from the *Kedushah*
The ultimate goal is to create a maximum distance from the *Sitra A'hra* (negative force), and closeness to the *Kedushah*

קו
Kav
Ray – Line
Ray of light that emerged from the *Ein Sof* (infinite) and entered on one side of the *'"Hallal"* (vacant space)

קודשא בריך הוא
Kudsha Berikh Hu
Saintly and Blessed He is
קליפות

Klipot
Husks (negative forces)
The *Klipot* are the manifestation of the negative force

קלקול
Kilkul
Deterioration – Damage
Kilkul is the opposite of *Tikun* (rectification)

קמיע
Kmi'a
Amulet
Names, or combinations of names of angels, with special signs or incantations, written on parchment to protect or to invoke particular powers

רוח
Rua'h
Soul - Second level of the soul
Rua'h is the second level and is acquired before the next levels

רוחני
Ru'hani
Spiritual
A spiritual person will give importance to this higher meaning of things, and live in the path of rightness to strengthen himself constantly

רחל
Ra'hel
Ra'hel - Partsuf Nukvah
Partsuf Ra'hel is of the aspect of kindness

רמח"ל
Ram'hal
Initials of Rabbi Moshe 'Haim Luzzatto

רע
Ra'
Evil – Bad

רפ"ח נצוצות
Rapa'h Nitsutsot
288 sparks
See Nitsutsot

רצון להשפיע
Ratson Lehashpia'
Will to bestow
The will of the Creator is to bestow goodness on His creatures

רצון לקבל
Ratson Lekabel
Desire to receive
By his nature man is himself a *Keli* (recipient) with a will to receive without limits

רשימו
Reshimu
Imprint – trace
Imprint of the first light that remained inside

שבירת הכלים
Shvirat HaKelim
Breaking of the vessels
The seven lower *Sephirot* that could not hold the influx of their lights and broke

שבת
Shabbat
The seventh day, *Shabbat* corresponds to the seventh
Sephira; *Malkhut*

שורש
Shoresh
Root
Every thing and existence has its root in the higher
realms

שכינה
Shekhina
Divine presence
One of the names of G-od

שכר
Sakhar
Reward
The variable guidance is on the basis of justice,
reward and punishment and is dependant on the actions
of man
This guidance is by the linear *Sephirot*

שער
Sha'ar
Gate – Portal
Entrance to a dimension
 Gate to enter a knowledge

תא חזא
Ta 'Haze
Come see (pay attention)
Expression frequently used in the *Zohar*

תורה
Torah
The Kabbalah is the mystical and esoteric explanation of the *Torah*
All the profound secrets explained in the Kabbalah, are alluded in the letters, words and different stories narrated in the *Torah*

תחית המתים
T'hiyat ha Metim
Resurrection of the dead
Final goal of the six thousand years

תיקון
Tikun
Rectification or action
In Hebrew, the word "*Tikun*" has different meanings
It can be understood as reparation or rectification but also as function, relation or action

תפארת
Tiferet
Sephira (beauty)
Sixth of the *Sephirot*

תפילה
Tefilah
Prayer
The order of the *Tefilot* is based on the systems of ascension of the worlds, as explained in the Kabbalah

תפילות
Tefilot
Prayers

תרי"ג
Taryag
613
There are 613 veins and bones to man, similarly, there are 613 *Mitsvot,* 613 parts to the soul, and 613 lights in each *Sephira* or *Partsuf*, this number is not arbitrary, as there are important interrelations and interactions between them

www.ingramcontent.com/pod-product-compliance
Lightning Source LLC
LaVergne TN
LVHW091358210726
843527LV00001B/41